Praise for

THE SOUL OF ALL LIVING CREATURES

"Enjoyable and electrifying reading."

—*The Inquisitive Mind*

"An insightful affirmation of our love of animals."

—*Kirkus Reviews*

"Animal lovers will appreciate this tribute to the connection between humans and animals."

—*Booklist*

"*The Soul of All Living Creatures* is an inspiring, joyful, uplifting account of the magical bonds between humans and the earth's creatures. This book conveys a profound message: we are part of a larger web of life that we must honor, or risk grave consequences. Thank you, Dr. Virga, for reminding us of this crucial fact."

—**Larry Dossey, M.D., author of *Reinventing Medicine* and *One Mind***

"A beautiful, wise, and inspiring book that will greatly enrich your relationship with all the animals in your life, including the human ones."

—**John Robbins, author of *The Food Revolution* and *Diet for a New America***

"In his passionate and convincing book, Dr. Virga has taken our understanding of animals a great step further. He helps us see that they are not like us—they are very different—and through powerful and affecting anecdotes with a wide range of species, he shows us what we can learn from them, from acceptance to communication to spirituality. An important and overdue book, beautifully rendered and valuable for anyone who loves animals."

—**Jon Katz, author of *Dancing Dogs***

"*The Soul of All Living Creatures* by noted veterinarian and animal behaviorist Dr. Vint Virga profoundly delivers on what the title promises. His voice is both intimate and informative, and his collection of stories reads more like a compelling novel than an anecdotal collection. This book takes the reader from smiles to laughter to empathy and tears, then ultimately to a clear perception of how understanding animals can make us better human beings. This is a must-read not only for animal lovers but also for those looking to create a life of compassion for ourselves and others."

　　　　　—**Nancy Ellis-Bell, author of *The Parrot Who Thought She Was a Dog* and coauthor of *A Man for All Species***

The Soul of All Living Creatures

The Soul of All Living Creatures

What Animals Can Teach Us

About Being Human

Vint Virga, D.V.M.

B \ D \ W \ Y
BROADWAY BOOKS
New York

Published in the United States by Broadway Books, an imprint of the
Crown Publishing Group, a division of Random House LLC, a Penguin
Random House Company, New York.
www.crownpublishing.com

BROADWAY BOOKS and its logo, B \ D \ W \ Y, are trademarks of Random
House LLC.

Originally published in hardcover in the United States by Crown
Publishers, an imprint of the Crown Publishing Group, a division of
Random House LLC, New York, in 2013.

Library of Congress Cataloging-in-Publication Data
Virga, Vint.
    The soul of all living creatures/Vint Virga, D.V.M.—First edition.
        Pages cm
    Includes bibliographical references.
    1. Virga, Vint. 2. Veterinarians—Biography. 3. Veterinary medicine.
4. Human-animal relationships. I. Title.
    SF613.V57V57 2013
    636.089092—dc23
    [B]   2012035166

ISBN 978-0-307-71887-7
eBook ISBN 978-0-307-71888-4

Cover design by Eric White
Cover photography: Anton Renborg/Gallery Stock

First Paperback Edition

146442087

For Babe
and that day in the Japanese garden.

For Gigi,
to the edge of the universe and back.

The soul is the same in all living creatures,

although the body of each is different.

—Hippocrates

Contents

Author's Note

The stories I tell in these pages are true. A few of those mentioned have permitted me to use their real names. In all other narratives, the names and identifying details of those whom I write about—people as well as animals—have been changed in order to protect their privacy and maintain confidentiality.

Throughout the book I refer with intention to individual animals as "he" or "she" instead of "it," which is customary in our culture. The use of "it" when referring to animals draws a distinction between them and us and reinforces viewing them as objects rather than fellow beings. It is clear from all I have written here I believe passionately that all living creatures, animals and humans, are unique and individual beings. I leave it to the reader to decide for themselves, after reading these pages, which they feel is more appropriate.

Introduction

*Lots of people talk to animals. . . . Not very many
listen, though. . . . That's the problem.*
—Benjamin Hoff, *The Tao of Pooh*

I had done all that I could for him. Pongo lay on his side in
the run, a stack of threadbare blankets beneath him and jugs
of warm water swaddled at his sides. For close to an hour I'd
been struggling to get him stabilized, since that moment I'd
first caught sight of him as he was carried through the treatment room door. Even when I was tugged away to attend to
the stream of other patients who'd gathered that night just
inside our doors—a stoic coonhound I'd seen before who'd
stubbornly tangled with his seventh porcupine, a threesome
of cats who'd delightedly grazed on the children's collection
of Halloween chocolates, a raccoon with a snotty nose and
runny eyes I feared foretold of distemper, a Newfoundland
puppy whose paw had been stepped on, a robin stunned from
flying headlong into a plate-glass window, and the others
taking refuge on that bitter, stormy November night—my
thoughts still drifted back to Pongo.

He'd arrived at the height of the first wave of patients as the techs triaged each animal amidst a flurry of phone calls, frantic clients, and paperwork. Whisking past the blur of faces lined up against the waiting room walls, Pongo's owners, Claire and Turner Wallace—a graying professor and his stately wife decked out in their finest clothes for a night on the town—had shunned the gurney the techs rolled to their car. Instead, cradling the whole of his body in a makeshift sling formed by their arms, they maneuvered Pongo through the short maze of hallways leading from reception back to the clinic's treatment room, the hub behind the scenes where we did our most intensive work. Huddled arm in arm together in a growing puddle from their rain-soaked clothes, they stood behind me watching over my shoulder as I tended to their beloved dog.

Ready at hand on every wall surrounding us, tucked into cabinets and tightly packed on rows of shelves, stood most every foreseeable supply, device, and piece of equipment needed to care for our patients each night: sutures, bandages, catheters, needles, boxes of color-coded syringes, sterile packs of surgical tools, a curious array of oddly shaped instruments uniquely fashioned for animals' bodies, rows and rows of medicine bottles holding powders, injections, and pills— a state-of-the-art formulary of drugs designed to treat whatever ails the body. Within view on either side of us, the surgery suite and a row of runs stood at the ready whenever they were needed. And sprawled on his side before me lay my patient.

Pongo, a two-year-old flat-coated retriever, was the first hit-by-car victim of the night after dashing toward a poodle in a pickup passing by his home. His long black hair, tangled in mats from being thrust and dragged against the pavement, effused an odor of rain, oil, and asphalt. Yet, other than a few contusions and abrasions, I'd failed to find any signs of trauma. His lab work and X-rays were likewise unremarkable. At eighty-five pounds, his barrel chest and solid frame had served him well.

But despite these minor injuries, Pongo's body betrayed it was in crisis. Through the ear tips of my stethoscope, I listened to his heartbeat pound while my fingers searched for a matching pulse. Yet, running my hands along his veins, I could barely feel the faintest flutter. His pupils gazed beyond me unfocused. His shivering skin felt icy cold. In response to a moment's pressure from my thumb, his dry, ashen gums blushed a gloomy gray-pink. Pongo was in progressive shock, if from nothing more than the sheer concussion of his impact with the speeding truck.

As a doctor in the emergency room seasoned by four grueling years of practice, I had grown to trust my knowledge and skills. Eight years earlier, as a freshman in vet school—well before my first hospital rounds—I had learned that "animals don't walk on their X-rays," a maxim repeated by our professors to stress the limits of diagnostic tests. As I write these words now, thirty years later, that lesson has borne out time and again. Above all the tests we may run as doctors—ultrasounds, blood work, or MRIs—we must trust in our sense of touch, eyes, ears, and instincts.

As I stood next to Pongo, weighing our findings, the results of our tests suggested he should be fine. Yet, in spite of my searching, something was missing—a piece of the puzzle, a hidden clue—and I was at a loss to find it. I knew that the best I could do for my patient was simply to step back and give him some time. Time to respond to the meds for shock. To the steady flow of sustaining fluids dripping through the IV line. To the soothing warmth of a quiet bed waiting for him in a nearby run.

Turning to Dr. and Mrs. Wallace before I stepped away from Pongo's side, I saw in their faces not only their angst but also their bleary-eyed looks of exhaustion. Facing Pongo's mortality had clearly taken its toll on them.

So, promising to keep in touch with any changes in his condition, I nudged them home for a bit of rest. And leaving Pongo in the care of Melissa, our more-than-capable treatment room tech, I left to begin removing the quills from my old familiar coonhound friend.

Though I checked on Pongo from time to time, it was not until a few hours later—when both exam rooms were at long last empty and each of the patients I'd seen in them were nestled in cages or runs for the night or safely back at home tucked in their beds—that I could focus on him once again. After repeating a thorough exam from chest to belly and limb to limb, I stepped back a pace to take in the whole picture. If anything, his condition had worsened. Despite our aggressive supportive care, he lay on his side where I'd seen him last, indifferent to all we had done for him. Each breath he took was a labored effort—a familiar blend of rasping sighs and guttural moans I'd heard before in trauma patients. His eyes drooped half-closed with a far-off focus. His gums remained pale, though, I fancied, less gray. Though before he flicked his ears to the sound of my voice, now he lay oblivious when I crouched beside him and spoke his name. Despite my best efforts, I was losing my patient.

Facing Pongo at three a.m., with the lights turned low and the clinic hushed, I surrendered to my growing frustration and sank exhausted to the floor. Too tired to talk, I sat by his side, leaning my back against the wall, while I worked at updating medical records, a daunting foot-high stack of charts. While my left hand scribbled my thoughts onto paper as diagnoses and treatment plans, my right arm draped loosely on Pongo's chest, lifting and falling with labored breath.

As we shared those blankets in that dim-lit run, I imagined picking up on some vague shift in Pongo: a slight ease in breathing, a softer moan, a lean of his body imperceptibly closer. While I worked at my notes, what at first seemed just whimsy—barely more than a passing thought—in that hour became unmistakably real. I felt his pulse strengthen. His heart rate slowed. But most telling of all, he shifted his focus from some distant planet to there by my side. With the weakest of wags at the tip of his tail, he licked my hand as I spoke his name. In medical terms, he became more responsive. But, simply put in other words, Pongo grew present in body and spirit.

Pulling his chart from the stack by my side, I pored through the entries on each of those pages—lab tests, exam results, treatments given, technician notes. In spite of his sudden, remarkable change, I could find nothing in our care of Pongo that differed that hour from all those before. Nothing, that is, except for the time I spent sharing those blankets with him. With Pongo then nuzzling into my lap, I came to realize the obvious. It wasn't my medical knowledge or skills that had strengthened Pongo's will to live. Instead it was simply those moments we shared, a soft word spoken, a simple touch. Indeed, those seemingly small acts of caring, I have no doubt, saved Pongo's life.

That evening with Pongo twenty-three years ago forever changed the course of my life as a vet. How I look at the ties that bind me to animals—their roles in my life and mine in theirs—took on dimensions I had never known possible. Doors opened into a profound new reality that I had only glimpsed and begun to comprehend: a world of insights into behaviors and relationships. My role had evolved beyond that of doctor to student, philosopher, teacher, and therapist.

Since my earliest memories (I was maybe four or five years old), I've felt drawn to animals by some unexplained force. At holiday gatherings, my parents' dinner parties, or days around town—especially in crowds—I could be found somewhere out of the way, comfortably sitting alone on the ground with a cat in my lap or dog close at hand. Sometimes I'd talk to them, other times not. I was simply content to be with them in silence and escape all the pressure of being with people—words freely spoken with so much unsaid, unspoken meanings, hidden agendas. With animals, I felt at home. Their messages were clear and true. What mattered in those moments was nothing more than our relationship.

Yet, somewhere in the process of becoming wiser and growing up—classes in science and analytical thinking; bullies and best friends and lessons learned; the death of our first dog; bringing home a new puppy; parties and dances and kissing a girl; walking alone through the canyons near school or for miles on the beach, sorting everything out—*Why is physics so hard? Why is chemistry easy? Why can I not get that girl off my mind? What did she mean last night when she called me? Why does the moon look so orange tonight? It is because of pollution or just where it is in the sky?*—going off to college; living in the dorms; courses and field trips and countless exams—my sense of belonging with animals diminished. Though I still held those feelings, the bond, the attraction I felt merely being with them, I resolved I would best serve them being a doctor: diagnosing diseases, sewing up wounds, showing I cared with my mind and my hands. Until I met Pongo.

I left general medicine several years later—first the emergency room, then my own clinic. While my practice had thrived for those years in between and the challenge of difficult cases endured, I felt something was missing in most of my work. The best medical care, diagnostics, and treatment, while part of the picture left more unattended—the behavioral needs of my patients and clients. Wondering why I was an hour behind schedule, my technician would softly crack open the door to find me sitting somewhere on the floor with a cat in my lap or a dog sprawled beside me, discussing with clients their routines at home. The message was clear.

So, leaving our life in the Oregon foothills, my practice, and our friendships we'd formed through the years, my fiancée and I packed up and moved with our dog and three cats to follow our dreams—to practice (after residencies) as veterinary specialists, Tiffany in dermatology and me in behavioral medicine. And though we had both been in practice for years, the work we were meant for had just begun.

The Soul of All Living Creatures traverses the world I've discovered since then in behavioral-medicine specialty practice, considering all different species of animals, from leopards and whales to cats, dogs, and wolves. It delves into the lives of my clients and patients: the problems they've faced, how I've tended to them, where I have helped, when I have failed, and, perhaps most of all, the lessons I've learned. But this book is as much about people as animals. Exploring behaviors and traits that we share with all sorts of creatures, it endeavors to show what animals can teach us about our own lives. What can a whale say about how we listen? How can an ocelot help us notice more? What can a girl and her fearful cat show us about being sensitive to those that we love?

Through unlocking such mysteries of animal behaviors, we can open a door into our own lives for new insights, perspectives, and ways of being. And as much as we're willing, if we listen and notice and embrace what we all hold in common with animals, we can bring more meaning and fulfillment to our lives.

I
Connection

If all the beasts were gone, men would die from a great loneliness of spirit. For whatever happens to the beasts, soon happens to man. All things are connected.

—Ted Perry

From birth, even before we've begun to focus on what lies beyond our grasp, a world of strange and wonderful creatures gathers together to watch over us: soft bunny faces on plush baby blankets snuggle with us as we lie in our cribs; stuffed teddy bears with bow ties and peacoats stand at the ready to help ease our fears; animal alphabets, murals with monkeys, and paintings of elephants hang on our walls, inspiring us to think and dream and look beyond the world we know. And at last when it's bedtime, as we drift to sleep, Winnie-the-Pooh, Peter Rabbit, Babar, and a parade of storybook characters spring from the pages with lives of their own to become endearing childhood friends, their tales retold on countless evenings.

Though children may set aside these companions (except, perhaps, with the closest of friends) in their urgency to feel more grown up, as adults we very much interweave animals into the fabric of our lives, inspiring new symbols that still captivate us. The cars we drive and sports teams we cheer for invoke their image in using their names with visions of emulating some special trait: the stealth of *Tigers*, speed of *Mustangs*, sting of *Hornets*, or strength of *Bulls*. From the stalwart elk of the Hartford Group to the sleek, fluid borzoi of Alfred Knopf, icons of animals spark in our minds lasting impressions that span generations. In truth, who among us does not feel some longing—an impulse to walk out on life as we know it (if merely for only a week or two)—to flee to some destination down under simply by seeing the Qantas kangaroo?

What underlies this attraction to animals? *Why are we humans so drawn to them?* How is it that animals so touch our hearts merely by naming them, seeing their picture? Why do their images echo inside us, move and inspire us to dare dreaming bigger, leaving impressions for most of our lives? Is the grip they hold on us cultural programming instilled by logos and ad campaigns or, perhaps, just a matter of constant exposure, beginning at the earliest age?

I believe our connection is rooted much deeper: lit by a spark before childhood memories, more profound than a yearning for superhuman traits, beyond the comfort we find in their touch, their listening ears, or their steady gaze.

What I see in their eyes is my own reflection and a sense that we share more than we recognize. The people and creatures I see in my practice share a bond that defies any logic or reason that explains what it is that they do to our lives. As I sit in between them and look back and forth from human to animal, in a very real sense I am watching a struggle that has occupied humans since our species began.

Outside the village of Vallon-Pont-d'Arc in the Rhône-Alpes region of southern France, the Ardèche River flows through sheer cliff canyons flanked by muted gray limestone walls. On a narrow terrace overlooking the valley lies the entrance to the Grotte Chauvet, a vast primordial underground cavern that shelters some of man's earliest art. Once a lair for Stone Age cave bears (the size of modern Kodiak bears), Chauvet in its floor holds their paw marks and scratches and is littered with bony remains of their prey.

As we look to the walls a different picture unfolds. Trekking back from the ledge lined with scrub oak and ivy and into the mountain for a quarter of a mile, through a labyrinth of breathtaking chambers and galleries, is like plunging backward into the last ice age. Well after the cave bears abandoned the cavern for the tundra and steppe with spring in full bloom, the earliest humans ventured into Chauvet for some unknown reason and left a collection that transcends all time between then and now. Each painting, now thirty thousand years old, in its own right is a masterpiece—strikingly rich in style, depth, and form—which viewed together capture scenes from a world that footprints, pawmarks, fragments of bones, and carbon dating can't begin to convey.

More than four hundred animals that then roamed the continent—with one human figure, a Venus, in their midst—come to life on the walls singly and in panels. But beyond their artistry, what separates them from their brethren found in other caves lies in which creatures the artists portrayed. Aside from the prey then most hunted by humans (reindeer, horses, ibex, and bison), the walls feature many more dangerous species—lions, rhinos, cave bears, and panthers, among other predators that once roamed outside. Yet, what stands out clearly and, perhaps, is most telling of what brought these artists inside Chauvet, is that the paintings do not depict a fear of these creatures, but instead celebrate their vitality.

The blink of her eyes in a horse's expression. A thrust of a rhino's head threatening to charge. The outward stare of a pride of cave lions, furtively stalking and ready to pounce. Scraping layers of clay to uncover the limestone, sketching and adding dimension in charcoal, painting in pigments with nuance and shading, the artists inspired their creatures to life. In the flickering torchlight, with blackness around them and their breath alone breaking the silence of the cave, the painters descended the depths of the earth to focus their vision on animals: their behaviors and patterns, the life force within them, and a sense of the deep-rooted kinship we share. In spite of a rock slide ten thousand years later that cached them in rubble for twenty thousand more, these paintings convey Chauvet's sacred importance as a place where man pondered his connection with animals.

Around the world, from culture to culture, our histories, traditions, and lifestyles as humans intrinsically mingle with animals' lives and many times depend upon them—for giving us food, clothing our bodies, and hauling our belongings around the countryside. Yet, at the end of the day, once their roles are fulfilled, we still feel a sense of connection to them. That perennial place that they hold in our psyche, the strength of their image we cherish as symbols, the parts that they play day-to-day in our lives: All exist because of our kinship with them. As our ancestors found in the Grotte Chauvet, we are drawn to bring animals into our lives because we see ourselves reflected in them.

Though, no doubt, the creatures we see now are different from those that once roamed the steppes outside Chauvet, it seems we are no less beguiled by their presence. Nearly two out of every three American families currently share their homes with pets. This amounts to an impressive 90 million cats, 74 million dogs, 151 million fish, 13 million reptiles, 16 million birds, and 24 million small mammals of sorts. Joining this impressively popular tribe, four million families own one or more horses, with three out of four horses living steps from their doors.

Reaching much further than the walls of our homes, we thrill at the chance of finding wildlife in nature. Impressions of paw prints emerge from the brambles, wander across our path, and lead off into the shadows. A fresh pile of scat with a few tufts of fur buzzes with flies at the edge of the trail. Claw marks in tree trunks so deep we can't fathom the strength of a bear with the swipe of her paw command our attention. *Dare we go further?* Due caution forewarns us . . . but the thought is enticing.

Craving more contact than we find in nature, 143 million guests flock to zoos and wild animal parks each year in North America. On paved-road safaris through mock African savannahs, dark winding trails in lush aviary glens, and footpaths weaving back and forth between a maze of habitats past impalas, kangaroos, zebras, and bears, we at last catch a glimpse of our favorite creatures, even if we stand apart behind a fence or across a moat.

On a drive up the freeway to a conference in Boston, I smile as my mind drifts to what lies ahead—not as much to the meetings as where I'll be staying—a chance to return to a favorite haunt, the Fairmont Copley Plaza Hotel. My delight in this grand old dame lies not in her history or stately decor, but instead in my times spent there with an old friend. The first time I entered the hotel lobby, Catie greeted me with the same doe-eyed look I've come to expect every time I see her. Raised as a puppy since seven weeks old to serve as a guide dog for the blind, she came to the Fairmont as a two-year-old Lab after a screening before her adoption revealed a small cataract in her left eye. Though her vision then, as now, was essentially sound—aside from the tiniest error, at times, when tracking a ball tossed high in the air—it disqualified her as a Seeing Eye dog. Hired as the Copley Plaza's canine ambassador, with an email address, appointment book, and business cards of her very own, Catie commands a devoted clientele for jogs to the commons, walks round the square, or strolls through the shops of Newbury Street. For me, my day just seems to flow better knowing most times I end up in the lobby, there's a good chance I'll find her there patiently waiting—ready to offer a welcoming wag, a kindhearted face, and a tummy for petting.

A travel-weary, bedraggled couple, spent from their flight and with bags still in hand, set all aside to crouch down by Catie and linger awhile, petting her on the rug before, at long last, going up to their room. A middle-aged man in a trim business suit on his way to a meeting room somewhere downstairs risks wrinkles and dog hair on his pants, sleeves, and coat in exchange for a moment to nuzzle with her. The flush, tear-stained cheeks of a young red-haired girl—perhaps five years old—not wanting to go home break with a smile as Catie leans into her arms. As I watch from a corner, in the course of an hour, a stream of admirers shower Catie with affection. With an open-armed ease saved for familiar friends, they speak to her with blissed squeals of excitement, cooing oohs and baby talk, and softly murmured confidences. Furrowed brows wrinkled with worry and stress softly melt as her eyes meet theirs and she gazes at them with unguarded acceptance. One after another, the change is uncanny.

We reach out to people as well as animals out of a longing we hold deep within to not be alone, to share what we feel, to relate in some way to the world around us. We yearn to be accepted for who we are, warts and all. We spend much of our lives in an unfolding saga, sorting among all the others we meet to find those who we believe best understand us, with whom we can feel free to just be ourselves. Yet with animals, I find, we do so quite differently.

By their sides we let down our guard and show them more of who we are.

Within the shelter of our own homes, one-half to two-thirds of us look on our pets as full-fledged family members. We speak of our pets as if they're our children, invite them into our beds with us, celebrate their birthdays, take them on vacations, and even chat to them on the phone as we leave messages on the answering machine. While we all talk to animals in one way or other, an astounding 94 percent of us speak to them as if they were human. And more than 90 percent affirm that our pets indeed respond in turn to our human fancies, emotions, and moods. By the same token, just as many believe our pets share human personality traits, such as being inquisitive, outgoing, or shy. Considering how we regard our connection with them, perhaps it's not surprising at all that slightly more than half of us would willingly risk our lives for our pets, and even more believe that our pets would devotedly rescue us.

Based on the findings from a recent survey, should fate somehow leave us for the rest of our days on an island living with one single companion, most of us would choose a dog or cat above a human (stranger, family, or even best friend). Perhaps even more telling, when asked, "Who listens to you best?" almost half of us confess that we feel most heard by our animal companions. And yet, though these may seem remarkable statistics, from the close bonds I've forged with my clients through the years—the stories they've shared, the relationships I've studied, the ties that I've witnessed between people and their pets—I simply accept them as a matter of truth.

Why would we choose to spend the rest of our lives with a pet as our partner instead of a person? How does an animal, simply with their presence, bring us more comfort than the arms of a friend? Why do we feel other species listen better, understand our emotions, and attend to our feelings more than our fellow human beings do?

I believe the answers to these questions lie in the sense of belonging we feel in the company of other creatures. In the presence of animals, we find true acceptance. Unlike with our peers, we feel no need to explain ourselves. Alone with them, our self-consciousness dissolves. With radios turned up as we drive down the freeway, we croon, trill, or belt out our songs with abandon, mindless of our dog panting in the seat behind us. Stepping from the shower to dry ourselves on the bathroom mat, we stand stark naked toweling off despite the gaze of our loitering cat. Upset and shaken by a fight with a friend, with our dog in our lap closely snuggled in our arms, we let the tears roll down our cheeks and confess to them where we went wrong.

We trust less conditionally in the bonds we share with animals. Unfettered by the judgments of others, in their silent presence we feel free to be ourselves. In place of solutions or answers to our questions, we gratefully welcome their quiet attention. Whether joining them in silence or relying on our words, we sense their regard for our thoughts and feelings. And we respond to our animals in kind.

Each day in my practice, I witness this kinship tested and proven strong time and again. Perhaps even more than with medical issues, the behavioral concerns that lead my clients to me challenge the very essence of what binds them to their animals. The zookeeper ambushed each day by the emu and the client whose cat howls all through the night share a desire to heal the bond that, somehow, has changed from what it once was. In their stories, filled with hours of struggles and worries, I hear their devotion to care for their animals. The lines on their faces and the look in their eyes convey without words the connection they share and how precious it is to them in their lives.

Regardless of how many years I have practiced, the faces of clients often linger in my thoughts not for the details involving their cases, but instead for the bond they shared with their animals and the lessons they taught me about that connection. Among those I've worked with who come to mind often, William and Margaret Robinson stand out for their selfless acceptance of their beloved Prudence and the ties they shared through the course of her life.

I'd first met the Robinsons at their front door after they'd called less than one week before, desperate to see me as soon as they could. It appeared from their story, as Margaret explained, that Prudence, their twelve-year-old calico cat, had switched personalities just overnight, though she'd never done so before in her life. After a week though, she hadn't changed back—not that they'd really believed she would—and Margaret and William didn't know what to do.

"It's not getting better. And Will is so patient."

I could hear him clear his throat on the other extension.

"Well, he is," Margaret said a little more softly, as if taking me aside to share her concerns.

Standing at their front door, as they ushered me in, I wasn't quite certain what to expect, although I'd read through their history twice. A small Tudor cottage they'd lived in for years on a lesser used side street up on College Hill, not far from the school where Margaret taught. Coatrack in the corner. Cat toy on the rug. No sign of Prudence in the hallway or beyond. But most cats didn't rush to greet me at the door.

Coffee and muffins waited on the table as we walked into the living room. And so did Prudence—certainly not hiding—lounging aloofly in an overstuffed armchair, considering me from the opposite corner. The waves of orange and black markings on her face blurred much of what I could read of her expression, though she appeared unperturbed and rather indifferent to my barging in on her midmorning rest. Still mindful, as always, of first impressions, I leafed through the medical records in her file, but nothing in her manner struck me as peculiar. Cats often feign benign disinterest of me (or other strangers) in their homes. Yet Prudence's calm belied the tale they told.

As an art dealer, William often traveled abroad—sometimes being away from home for months at a time—mostly in England, the Netherlands, and France. Margaret, an art teacher at a private school, stayed back at home during most of Will's trips, flying to join him in London or Paris only for short trips once in a while. Although their daughters, Bridget and Abby (now both in their thirties), had moved out in college, they still lived in town and often dropped by to keep Margaret company when Will was abroad.

On a trip to New Hampshire twelve years before, Margaret and Will had come upon Prudence on a quick run to the grocery store. The smallest of three girls in a litter of six, huddled in a corner of old cardboard box, she'd grabbed Will's attention right there on the spot. Sending Margie on in to get fresh bread and milk, Will knew as he talked to the boy and his mom that the shy, tiny kitten was perfect for him. Back out of the store with a bag in her arms, seeing Will still enchanted, Margaret agreed.

Apart from the litter, the demure, quiet kitten molted her shell into a tomboyish girl—loving and sweet, but always underfoot (or else, they would learn, into some sort of mischief). Now, twelve years later, she was still quick and playful. Her favorite game was retrieving hair scrunchies that Will shot from his fingers like a rubber band, which she could play off and on all afternoon. But, still being older and not quite as active, she was equally fond of a nice, warm lap into which she could curl up and doze for an hour. Though friendly with visitors, especially their daughters, Will was her favorite, no ifs, ands, or buts. Whenever he was home, she was his constant companion, following him from room to room—not clingingly like glue but faithfully nearby.

Two weeks ago, though, when Will returned from Amsterdam after being on the road for most of May and June, Prudence had within a day transformed into a different cat. William had arrived in the middle of the night after a misconnected flight, happy to be finally home, but jet-lagged and exhausted. Margaret had waited up, first baking cookies then reading in bed, but by midnight had drifted off to sleep despite her best intentions. When William tiptoed in at last just as the clock struck two a.m., Prudence, as always, trotted up to greet him at the first crack of the door. Purring in her older cat, raspy sort of way, and nuzzling against his legs as he tried to walk, Prudence insisted she should be first and Will could attend to his bags after her. Happy to be welcomed home, especially at that time of night, William gratefully collapsed with Prudence and stretched out with her on the living room rug.

After a good long cuddle and pet (Will guessed five minutes, but he could have dozed off), he returned to his luggage to retrieve his toothbrush and a pouch of jerky treats for Prudence he'd stuffed somewhere in between his clothes. Admittedly digging through the bag a bit roughly, raking shirts and underwear out onto the floor, he dropped a loosely tied sack of beads—a present for his granddaughters to string into necklaces, bracelets, and such. Startled by the mass of little balls hitting the floor like a hailstorm, Prudence took off like a flash down the hall.

Not too surprising. *But poor Pru,* Will thought. So, once he'd tidied up the mess, Will followed down the hallway to see where Prudence fled and make sure she was calm again. But, after checking underneath the bed, behind the dresser, in the corner by the desk, and even in the shower stall without finding Prudence, Will at last gave up and, lying down by Margaret's side, surrendered to exhaustion.

"And then, that morning when I got out of bed, it was

like I woke up in the Twilight Zone," he said with a smile while he shook his head.

"I remember seeing Prudence as I walked to the bathroom. She was sitting in the hall just outside the door—not really anything unusual, though. She sometimes does that first thing in the morning.

"So, anyway, I showered and shaved and dressed in my robe. And it was then, when I stepped back out, that the hairs went up on the back of my neck. Prudence hadn't moved an inch. And she was staring at me like I'd never seen."

He paused for a moment and cleared his throat.

"I think I said, 'Hey, Pru—it's me,' as I started walking toward her and the bedroom door. Then she hissed and growled and even spat—and after that, of course, I froze."

I waited in silence for a couple of moments, and then nudged him on, asking, "So what did Pru do then?"

"Well, it really didn't seem to matter. She kept on hissing and her fangs looked huge. That probably sounds silly, but it really was true. And her pupils were so big and dark. She looked like she was . . . well, in a way possessed.

"So, I called out to Margie and I stood really still."

"And I'd already heard something crazy going on. So, I was on my way to Will to find out what was happening. But as soon as I reached Prudence, she ran past me down the hall."

Twice later that day and many more times since, William found himself cornered one place or another—in the kitchen, bedroom, bathroom, or study—with Prudence at the doorway not allowing him to move. Any attempt he made to pass was met with even more horrific growls and, if he dared go farther, Prudence started screaming and swatting.

"And never toward Margaret, only you?"

Will nodded.

"Oh, Prudence runs every time she hears me coming— but only when she's in one of those states. Otherwise, she's her normal self with me," Margaret added to help explain.

"So, when Margaret's away at school and you're here alone . . ."

"I carry a broom wherever I go. Oh, I don't hit her with it; I just hold it out in front of me. But as long as I have it, I can keep her at a distance. And then I can manage to slip on by her."

"What then? Doesn't she just follow you and trap you somewhere else?"

"Sometimes."

I looked at William with his wrinkled brow. Confusion? Resignation? A bit of both? I couldn't tell. But his eyes said it all to me—the bewildering sadness of his cat attacking him, the bitter loneliness of missing his friend.

What could be done to help them depended upon my diagnosis. In most respects, Prudence's story fit the mold of a cat with redirected aggression. Some cats, once upset by one thing or another, can react ever after that, instead, to something else. In essence, it's a matter of a poorly made association. The beads, for Prudence, were the villains that had upset her; but Will, in happening to be nearby, became the understudy in their absence. But while, in my mind, the story fit quite well, a queasy feeling in my gut nagged that it was something else. And through my years of practice, I have learned to trust that instinct. So, before we even dove into the steps of behavioral management, I recommended that we get her in to see a neurologist as quickly as possible.

Tragically, my suspicions were confirmed. The beads were not the cause of her behavior. The aggression to William, nothing more than an odd quirk, proved an ill omen of what lay ahead. Prudence had a meningioma, a brain tumor sometimes found in older cats, which once in a blue moon shows up first as odd behavior. These tumors, made up of connective tissue cells, are usually benign, so they really don't spread to other parts of the body. But in this case, benign does not mean good, for though the cells don't move, they continue to multiply, pushing out and rubbing ever harder on their neighboring cells, like a pebble in a shoe pressing on our foot to cause a sore. And as the tumor grows with nowhere else for it to go, more and more of the healthy brain gets squeezed and damaged by the uncontrolled cells. Which is just what had happened in Prudence's brain. And in the next six months, Prudence's health worsened, slowly and steadily, bit by bit, until in the end there was no other decision but for Will and Margaret to ease her passing.

As I write down these words now many years later, the heartbreaking details we dealt with back then pale when compared to the bond that they shared. Even at the worst of times, when William was attacked six or seven times a day, before and after the diagnosis, they offered Prudence only kindness and returned her aggression with sensitivity.

Perhaps the power that enabled William Robinson to

overcome his fear and shock at Prudence's attacks is the same power that brought Pongo to recover on that blanket. I believe that a force exists intrinsically in all of us and has existed since the dawn of man. It is born from the kinship we share with other creatures. It's what draws us to them in images and sounds and what brings us comfort when we seek them out. It's what inspired the artists of Chauvet: what they pondered in the darkness of the cavern and their souls. When we reach out to animals, we embrace a part of our human nature that's as vital to us as our hearts and minds, and that connection stirs our spirit to transcend the limits of what we think is possible, to become even more than we believe we are. And it begins by looking outward, away from ourselves, to the animals around us.

2

Sensitivity

One often hears of a horse that shivers with terror, or of a dog that howls at something a man's eyes cannot see, and men who live primitive lives where instinct does the work of reason are fully conscious of many things that we cannot perceive at all. As life becomes more orderly, more deliberate, the supernatural world sinks farther away.

—William Butler Yeats

For the last half an hour, while I listened to the Parkers relate their story of the past few months, Sabrina stretched cozily by Matthew's side, just at the other end of the sofa. Through half-closed eyelids, drifting in and out of sleep, and ever so softly purring off and on, she stirred now and then to consider me with mild interest. Just across the table in an old leather armchair, Rosalind stretched comfortably in Angela's lap and preened her thick black mane and coat in long, sweeping strokes with the barbs of her tongue, while Angie teased out a couple of mats from beneath her ears with a wire brush. With the glow of flames from the freshly stoked fire, toys tucked tidily into a chest, and mugs of steaming cocoa on the table just in front of us, the scene was very much idyllic—almost out of a storybook—and the tension I felt from my rush to arrive seemed to melt from my shoulders and then drift off.

Though, in point of fact, the cats weren't siblings, Angie and Matt had adopted them both on the same day five years earlier from a small rural shelter in upstate New York. Barely ten weeks old at the time, amidst the chaos of mingled litters—with the bravest ones nudging forward to be scratched—little Sabrina and Rosalind so devotedly clung to the couple that the Parkers gave in to returning home with both to complete their newly formed family. In the time that it took Matt to drive back to Brooklyn, with both kittens tuckered out side by side on a plush downy blanket stuffed inside their crate, the two had become devoted sisters. Adjusting to life in the city as indoor cats without a hitch, in a matter of days the kittens had laid claim to every nook and corner of the Parkers' flat. With space being tight in the neat, cramped apartment and one or another forever underfoot, sitting in the empty chairs at breakfast time and dinner, nudging beneath the blankets in the middle of the night, or digging in the litter box while humans used the toilet, all learned to share the flat equally.

A couple of years later with the cats then fully grown, Angie and Matt began trying in earnest to add another member to the family. Though Sabrina and Rosalind had mellowed as they grew, the conditions of their life tucked together in the flat had shifted from cozy to uncomfortable. When a two-bedroom co-op straight across the park with

twice as much room and a view opened up, the Parkers leapt
with gusto for the larger place to nest. And as before, though
with much more space to share, the cats adjusted blithely to
their brand-new home, graciously accepting each and every
room as theirs.

Fast-forward twelve months, when the couple came home
from the hospital with baby Mia cradled in their arms, and
the cats seemed curious but mostly unimpressed with the
newest addition to their family. Accustomed as kittens to
living in close quarters, they shared the extra bedroom with
the baby generously. Whether Mia nursed with Angie in her
rocking chair, changed diapers on the dresser while her daddy
sang her songs, napped in her crib, or cried plaintively all
night, the cats were only too willing to supervise from the
nursery rug.

The first hints to Angie that there might be a problem
appeared only recently, when Mia turned three or a little
before then, give or take a month. In those years in between,
both cats honored their duties, keeping tabs on the baby as
she toddled then walked. But Angela wondered as Mia grew
older and became independent and strong if Sabrina—just
maybe—felt she was less needed or even a third wheel with
Mia and Roz. For while Rosalind steadfastly kept up with
Mia and devotedly stayed by her side night and day, Sabrina
seemed to grow a bit reserved. More and more at story time,
and then at other times of day, Sabrina would leave Rosalind
to chaperone, while she withdrew to Matt and Angie's room
on her own to snuggle in her favorite nest beneath their

king-size bed. And finally, just a few weeks ago, as her absence grew painfully obvious, Matthew took Sabrina to their family vet.

In spite of a thorough physical exam and a full set of tests that were sent to the lab, "She seems to be healthy," Dr. Stouffer confessed. She could find nothing medically wrong with Sabrina. In fact, she appeared to be in excellent health, having gained a pound since her most recent visit, barely six months earlier. Clearly, in spite of her seclusion in the bedroom, she'd managed to eat quite heartily. Still convinced that Sabrina's change was meaningful, but at an utter loss to offer any reason why, Dr. Stouffer recommended that they call me at my office.

The image of a reclusive cat huddled beneath a king-size bed clashed with the one just a few feet away. While she peacefully dozed on the sofa by Matthew, I mulled over the reasons that might explain this standoffish twist in Sabrina's behavior: sounds of construction from the neighboring building; noises of sirens or traffic outside, or maybe of passing dogs barking and baying; an electric device in the nursery or elsewhere—baby monitor, toys, humidifier, radio—tensions with Angela, Matthew, or Mia; conflict between her and Rosalind; or perhaps some vague illness, still silent and brewing. While I sat on the sofa with this differential, weighing each likelihood with all that I'd heard, the answer at once became all too apparent.

With a burst of shrill giggles and a flurry of footsteps, the front door flew open as Mia returned with a young blond-haired woman I guessed was her nanny. Shedding her coat in a blur of excitement and flicking her rain boots off onto the floor, Mia ran to her mommy and tugged on her arm, insisting on sharing her adventures of the morning. While Matt introduced me to their helper, Nanny Kate, and Mia recounted a game that she'd played with her best friend, Sophie, in the rain at the park, I discreetly kept an eye on the cats. Though awake and alert from the noise and the bustle, they both looked content as they rested unfazed. Likewise, when Mia ran up to her daddy, still telling her story while nuzzling up and wrapping her arms around his neck in a hug, Sabrina, though watchful, didn't seem too concerned.

It was not until Mia turned her focus to the cats, with joyous squeals of "Kitty!" as she forgot to end her tale, that I saw what I needed to confirm my suspicions. In an instant Sabrina braced all of her body. Tucking herself in a tight little bundle and turning her gaze through those squinting green eyes to me with a pitifully doleful expression, she endured the affection as best she could. But the instant that Mia ran over to Rosalind (with equal affection for both of her cats), Sabrina instinctively seized her good fortune and swiftly but silently fled from the room.

After asking her parents to wait back with Mia, I quietly traced where Sabrina's path led. True to what Matthew and Angie had told me, I found her nestled in a burrow far beneath the bed, tucked in between an assortment of boxes. As I lay on the rug with the bed skirt draped on me, she eyed me intently with quiet regard. When I made no attempt to lure or retrieve her, after another minute or two, she rested her head on an old pair of slippers. And as we both lay there, calmly watching each other, we listened to giggles and shrieks of delight from where she'd escaped, now directed toward Rosalind.

When I returned to the family a few minutes later, Mia danced by, shuffling off to the nursery, with Rosalind placidly draped in her arms. Given that image and all that I'd seen, the cause of Sabrina's behavior was clear. Yet, since Angie and Matt had never mentioned their daughter's keen zeal for their cats, I considered how best to broach what I'd noticed.

"I can see," I began, looking back toward the nursery, "that Mia truly adores both her kitties.

"So, I was just wondering," I said after a pause, "how often does she really get a chance to play with them?"

As I reached for my cup and sat back in the sofa, I was fully unprepared for Angie's response. "Oh, she follows them constantly, day in and day out, whenever she's home—well, whenever she can."

When I turned to their nanny, who had joined us from the nursery, she nodded discreetly with an understanding glance.

"But apart from when she returns from adventures—her walks in the park, playdates, and such—how often is she this excited to see them?"

Angie's reply, quite simply put, stunned me. "Are you kidding? It's like that pretty much all day long."

As I sat for a moment and let her answer sink in, I felt the full weight of Sabrina's dilemma. It was easy for me to empathize with my patient. With a devoted admirer (one who looked like a giant) chasing me tirelessly from morning to night—not to mention, quite often, with loud squeals of pleasure—I, too, would desperately want to escape.

"Between the two cats, does she have a favorite?"

"Not really." Matt shrugged, and then added with a smile, "Though most often, I'd say she ends up with Roz."

Noticing the nursery was eerily quiet, I asked, "Could we peek at what they're up to right now?"

Without hesitation, they offered, "Of course!" while standing together and leading the way.

Looking in from the doorway, I could not help but smile at the storybook scene playing out in the room. With a blanket wrapped around her like a posh winter coat, Rosalind lay comfortably purring on the rug. Across from her sat Mia, primly pouring cups of pretend tea. Completing the circle sat two favorite dolls, a velvet Peter Rabbit and a well-worn teddy bear. And in the center between all her special tea guests, Mia had properly laid out a spread with mock jars of jams, biscuits, cookies, and bread.

While we took in the scene with amusement and pleasure, I could only marvel at Rosalind's poise. With her soft, rumbling purrs and a placid expression, she clearly delighted in all the attention. Yet what touched me more was her good-natured deference to each of young Mia's fancies and whims. All at once, then, it struck me: Roz took on the role of deftly deflecting attention away from her sister when Mia wanted to play. And though I admit I cannot know for certain, as I grew to know Roz in the following months, I believe she did so with selfless intention, acting out of kindness and compassion for her sister.

As Matt, Angie, and I joined the group on the rug, I tried to convey Sabrina's perspective. Explaining how squeals, play, and even affection can sometimes be quite daunting to a small cat, I suggested a way to encourage Sabrina to join with the family more comfortably. We decided to name the new game "whisper kitty." Each time that Mia wished to play with Sabrina, she would speak very softly—in the quietest voice imaginable—and then wait to see how Sabrina responded. If she left, so be it; if she didn't, they'd reward her by gently tossing treats to her. In place of all her lavish hugs, Mia would offer the wisp of a touch—the lightest of strokes to her forehead or back—as a way of giving Sabrina her love.

"Most kitties," I offered, "are much more perceptive and sensitive than we might even imagine." Impassioned cuddles and kisses are human—not traits we see in the feline world. And though many cats adore being snuggled, a soft voice and gentle touch are better for others. More than just giving love, *expressing* our love calls for sensitivity to how others perceive what we're offering them.

Shifting their focus onto Sabrina, I pointed out how, in spite of her hiding, she wanted to stay with the family. Even with Mia's abounding élan, Sabrina contentedly lay where she was until she had no choice but to be hugged. So to better encourage Sabrina to stay wherever the family may be in the house, we would set up safe resting spots in several places. With cat beds and pillows just beyond Mia's reach—on dressers, cabinets, and upper bookshelves—Sabrina could rest undisturbed while also being closer to the family.

As I put on my coat when it was time to leave, I worried how the Parkers and their kitties would fare with the changes they'd be making in the coming weeks. Though I had little doubt we could help Sabrina, our success depended most upon their sensitivity. How earnestly would they try on a cat's perspective? Would they adjust their lives enough to help Sabrina feel secure? For Mia, could this new way of showing affection nurture the passion she felt for her kitties? I knew the coming weeks would tell.

One month later, after knocking at their door, I stood sweeping snow from my overcoat as I nervously waited for someone to answer. Try as I did, it was hard to imagine how they had managed with all of our plans and what our next steps would be if we had failed. Knowing this morning I'd visit at naptime, I wasn't surprised when Matt opened the door and whispered hello without Angie beside him. Admittedly though, as I gave him my coat and we walked from the entryway into the hall, I struggled to make out his facial expression. Then just as we passed it, the nursery door opened; Angie stepped out and reached for my hand.

I could feel the tears welling as I stood in the doorway. Mia lay sound asleep in her bed. That peaceful look of her face on the pillow reminded me of my own daughter's that morning, as I left before dawn to catch the first train. Down by her legs, among folds of blankets, Sabrina and Rosalind nestled side by side, sleepily watching us through half-shut eyes.

The three of us stood there in silence together only a minute or so, I would guess, listening to the tick of the clock; the faintest hint of a now-and-then purr; and the soft, murmured breathing of a three-year-old sleeping. Then I felt a tug gently on my sleeve, and I followed Angela into the hall.

As we sat in the kitchen and Matt brewed some coffee, I learned how Mia, with almost no coaching, had embraced my advice with that sense of adventure she brought to all that she did with her cats. The effect on Sabrina was swift and dramatic. Almost at once, they noticed when Mia would play with her toys in the living room, Sabrina began to linger nearby and watch from her perch on an upper bookshelf. With Mia speaking in the softest of voices along with some generous coaxing with treats, over time Sabrina crept from her roost down to the floor, more comfortably hovering closer and closer.

Excited by the changes that she saw in Sabrina, Mia took the game of "whisper kitty" further than we'd planned— talking softly to her parents when she wished to make a point, dressing up dear Rosalind a bit less in her games, and tiptoeing around the house at most times of the day.

Rosalind, too, became even more present, not just in body but also in mind. To both Matt and Angie she seemed more relaxed and content with Sabrina once again by her side. When Mia was gone, they spent more time together and when she was home they took on their old roles as nannies (or maybe, perhaps, more as chaperones). And the other night, once Mia was dressed in jammies and ready for bed, the two cats, as a pair, followed her to the nursery. Then while

Matt tucked her in and began his story, Roz and Sabrina both jumped in the bed. And the three fell asleep curled up side by side.

Sensitivity is a state of being aware and responsive to our world and those around us, as well as to ourselves. More than observing, for us to be sensitive we must grasp from each moment as much as we can. To do so, of course, we must draw from our senses—what we see with our eyes, hear with our ears, touch, taste, and smell, even feel in our gut—and bring these together to form an impression of what is occurring inside and around us. Yet our senses, indeed, don't paint the full picture but merely a fragment of all that exists.

Bats hunt for mosquitoes with sonar we can't hear as we watch them dart to and fro through the night. While we snuggle together watching a movie, our dogs see it more as a series of pictures flickering past when projected on the screen, more like the first silent films at the theater. When after a thunderstorm we gaze out our window at the brilliance of a rainbow as the sun breaks through the clouds, our cats view a pastel version missing reds and greens. Every species that exists has adapted their senses to view the world from a different perspective, unique from all others. And what we perceive from our vantage point determines how we experience our world.

Consider, for a moment, our neighbor's cat, Belinda, as she first wakes in the morning while her family still sleeps. In the early pre-light hours of dawn, with only the palest blush of purple beginning to color the eastern sky, she slips through her cat door, pads across the lawn, and fades into the shadows of the woods between our homes.

Watching from my office window, I hear nothing to betray her as she steals through the underbrush and brittle autumn leaves. With predator instincts—alert, watchful, patient— she wisely pays heed to each of her senses, as she lurks near the birdbath in consummate silence. Though I can barely make out their colors or forms, a pair of cardinals and several tree sparrows, perched in the branches a few feet above her, take turns at the feeder while regarding Belinda.

A glint of some movement grabs my attention. I turn to catch sight of a field mouse scrambling from the steps near the basement to somewhere below me. Though easily sixty feet away, Belinda's ears instantly twist in our direction. Leaping from her resting place, she nimbly sprints the twenty yards and neatly lands on our doorstep in seconds. Two seconds too late (as the mouse has since fled), her nose points uncannily toward the garage. But first she must sort through a mare's nest of past smells that mingle together in the port cochere—tires that have passed through, stacks of old herb pots, bags of freshly pulled grasses and weeds, tracks of our own feet, chipmunk and squirrel trails, piles and drifts of dry autumn leaves—all to which, though I live here, I'm oblivious. Yet, she discerns each with exacting precision.

She sniffs at the gap beneath the door to the garage (just large enough for a mouse to slip through) and stands frozen—a statue of pure concentration—for half a minute or longer; I'm not really sure. Then she looks back to the

driveway around her, scanning it for any small trace of movement. Perhaps because she spies me sipping from my mug,
or catches a waft of my tea in the breeze, she looks up to my
window. Meeting my gaze, she pauses a moment—we watch
from opposite sides of the window—and then Belinda saunters off, back to the woods to resume her hunt.

Living with sensitivity bids us to step out of our perspective and view the world as others do. When I was in my early
thirties, restless and searching for a meaning to life—during
the years my wife refers to fondly as my "monk stage"—one
particular weekend challenged the very core of my beliefs on
living with sensitivity.

During a three-day retreat I had joined for a few days of
thoughtful self-reflection, after returning from dinner one
evening, we were asked by the leader of our group to swap
shoes with another person. As we arranged ourselves around
the room at the end of a long day of soul-searching, I mar-
veled at the circle of faces in the softened light of our gathering place. Some eyes I knew well and, in turn, they knew me
from countless times we'd shared together—dinners spent in
each other's homes, meetings for tea in the afternoon, walks
in the park and on trails in the woods sharing tales and confidences, trips to the coast, movie dates, late-night talks underneath the stars, sharing hopes and dreams, regrets and fears,
and all the stuff that friendships are made of. Others I'd just
begun to know or, in some faces, I'd barely met—a smile, a
pause, a puzzled look—in some an untried meeting point, in
others a flicker of newfound connection. Before I'd settled on

anyone with whom I wanted to switch my shoes, Ian, who I'd known for years, walked up and asked me to join him. And even though I'd planned on pairing with someone less familiar, all the same I was grateful for the simple comfort of an old friend.

As we arranged ourselves around the room and sat on the rug to swap our shoes, something odd began to happen. Despite how well we knew each other from all the times we'd spent together, as I slipped off my shoes and he handed me his, I was struck by our differences. Much sturdier than me and a good foot taller, he was dressed in the same gear he wore to work—flannel shirt, blue jeans, leather belt, steel-toed shoes—a standard uniform, more or less, for an Oregon tree farmer. On the other hand, as usual when I wasn't dressed in surgery scrubs, I wore a camp shirt, khakis, and loafers. We settled into each other's shoes, and as I tugged at the shoelaces, my feet, to me, seemed amazingly small. Yet, despite their ill-fitted roominess, his shoes gave off a comfortable warmth, reflecting his body heat even after he had shed them.

Were my feet just chilled or were his so much warmer?

As I stood up to return to the group, his shoes transformed into leaden weights. To keep from stepping right out of them, I arched my soles and curled my toes—a memory of dress-up in Daddy's clothes and stomping through the bedroom. Standing, sitting, or walking about as the evening wore on and the hour got later, I began to notice my body shifting in the subtlest ways in how I behaved—how I stretched on the rug; how I crossed my legs; how I wiggled my toes as I spoke and listened; how I reached out to others and they to me with quirky, curious differences. And though knowing Ian as well as I did, I questioned how well I understood him.

An age-old Cheyenne proverb teaches, "Do not judge your neighbor until you have walked two moons in his moccasins." Until we step in another's shoes and truly get the feel of them, we can only imagine the world as they see it. Yet with feet in lieu of paws and hooves, how can we walk in an animal's shoes? In spite of our kinship and depth of connection, we are aliens to their world.

On walks through the neighborhood with our dog, Katie, I scratch my head and watch in wonder as she is drawn to lampposts one after another and sniffs at each with newfound fascination. While I stand by and cluelessly watch her, as much as I try to understand (and many times wish that we'd just move on), she is lost in a world I can only imagine. I envision a dog's world with clouds of aromas—some muted pastels, some lusciously brilliant, painted on tree trunks, seeping from crevices, and wafting aimlessly in the breeze. Enthralling. Alluring. Beguiling. Seductive.

If for just one day we could smell as a dog does, in what ways would that day differ from others? And how might we be changed afterward? Could we go on with our lives as before, ignoring all that our senses miss? Or would we then dare to look at the world from a fresh perspective?

Imagine, for a moment, walking into a large gathering at a friend's house, hotel ballroom, or perhaps a restaurant and instantly, with just a sniff or two, knowing more about the people around you. Who is nervous? Who's afraid? Who is excited and happy to greet you? Moving beyond a dog's perspective, how would it feel to surge through the waves and leap through the air with the ease of a dolphin? What would it be like to lope through the savannah, grasses billowing in your wake, in a coalition of cheetahs, moving toward a nearby grazing herd of impala? Or to swiftly glide through the cold autumn air as silently as a great horned owl, having spotted through the blackness of night the stripe of a skunk on the forest floor below you?

How, then, is it possible to step into the shoes of an animal? Simply put, as humans, we can't. But we can acknowledge our human condition and our remarkable differences as species. We begin to open to a new perspective by recognizing that we perceive only a fraction of all that surrounds us. Though we never see the atoms that make up our own fingertips, we know, nonetheless, that they exist, and our lives are intrinsically based on them. With electron microscopes, we can even manage to peek at them, to see the matter that we are made of. Likewise, knowing there are sounds beyond our range of hearing, colors and details our eyes simply miss, and aromas we breathe to which we are oblivious, we can turn to animals for fresh, new perspectives by envisioning the world as if we stood in their footsteps.

In the hurried pace of our daily routines, we all too often neglect to notice what our senses reveal to us. At the end of the day as we drive down the freeway, in our haste to make it home, we ignore the ochre hues of sunset fading before us between the clouds. With windows closed to the snarl of traffic and radios tuned to the evening news, we miss a flock of geese above us honking as they pass overhead and the cool smell of the evening breeze blowing past us across the pavement. Even when we make it home—while our dogs wag merrily at our heels as if we've been away for weeks and our cats jump to snuggle into our laps as we collapse upon the sofa—our thoughts often drag us right out of the moment, away from the comfort of being at home, the nuzzle of an adoring pet, the ease of familiar smells and sounds. Distracted by responsibilities and focused on our hopes and dreams, we neglect what is right within our reach. And in so doing, we miss the moment and all the rich experiences it offers us.

Dating back to the Han dynasty and spanning several religions since then, an ancient Chinese parable tells of three blind men and an elephant. One day, on their way to a far-off village, the three men were following a path through the jungle. As the trail wound down through a river gorge, they felt the ground begin to tremble and heard the crushing of branches and vines coming from the gulley that the path was surely leading to.

The oldest one doubted whether they should continue, but after talking among themselves, they all agreed to carry on. When at last the trail flattened again and they'd left the slope of the bluff behind them, the men crossed the path of a local herdsman, tending to his elephants while they grazed along the riverbank.

As soon as he saw the men approaching, the herdsman quickly called out to them, "Good day to you, travelers.

There's no need to be concerned. My elephants know this canyon well and are very used to all sorts of strangers."

Having never encountered an elephant, the three were naturally curious from countless tales they'd heard of them.

While the men fearlessly approached the stranger, the eldest one led and spoke up to explain, "All three of us are blind men, sir, and have never seen an elephant. And standing now so close to them, my friends and I are quite intrigued about the fascinating sounds that these creatures seem to make."

He paused for a moment to confer with his companions. The other two encouraged him to carry on, and so he asked, "Before we pass, since you work with these elephants—and, clearly, know them very well—may we ask you to describe them and tell us what they're doing now?"

Walking up to them, the herdsman replied, "I believe I can do even better than that." Holding out his arms to the older man, the herdsman said, "Come take my hands, if you are willing, and I will lead you up to one, so you can meet her for yourself."

Once the other two heard this offer, they stepped up quickly to the elder's side, and the three blind men walked in single file as the stranger led them to an elephant cow. Stopping a few yards from her side, the herdsman asked them to wait together until he brought her closer to them. As all three eagerly stood in silence, each imagined what he would soon find with an elephant standing by his very own side.

They could smell her breath and the scent of her skin as the cow stepped up and stood before them. Then, taking the first man by the hand, the herdsman led him to her closest leg. With a smile on his face and a grunt of fascination, the eldest lightly touched the elephant's leg and then more boldly groped to explore in widening swaths from her toes to her shoulder.

Returning to the other two, the herdsman took the next man's hand and quietly led him to the elephant's rear. There the second man caressed and examined every inch of her swishing tail, while the herdsman left to retrieve their friend.

Guiding the last one to the elephant's head, the herdsman led his hand toward the old cow's face. Grasping her ear with a look of enchantment, the third man softly cooed as he stroked her skin, and the ear, in response, flapped back and forth against him.

When each man felt satisfied with all that he had learned, the herdsman steered them back one by one to the trail, where they thanked him profusely and continued on their journey.

Though all three were quiet as they walked along the river, each man was eager to share all he'd discovered. At last, the eldest spoke up, saying, "I had always imagined elephants to be large and sturdy, which she certainly was. But I was awed by how much she was like a tree—tall, strong, and steady . . . yet remarkably soft."

"How very odd that you would say this," the third man said after hearing his friend. "You could not have been feeling the elephant! Oh, I agree, she was large and soft, but she was plainly more like a leathery fan. The breeze she made as she waved to and fro tickled my face while I held her in my hands."

After listening to all that the others said, the second man at last declared, "I'm not sure what either of you touched with your hands, but it quite clearly wasn't the elephant. She was not like a fan or a tall, sturdy tree. She had leathery skin that was wrinkled and bald, and a coarse tuft of hair at the top of her head. And with the way that she wriggled, she reminded me of a snake!"

They continued for miles down the river gorge trail, with each man describing the creature he had met. But with their portrayals each being so different, they found no way to reconcile them in the end.

And later that evening as they lay down to rest, the image of what they had held in their own hands was no more of an elephant than what they envisioned before they left that morning.

When we limit our experience to what we perceive, we let our senses define our existence. Unless we are willing to step out of our shoes to consider all that we may miss beyond what we are sensing, our lives become narrowed and circumscribed. Sensitivity is a process of always reaching out, beyond what we think we know, to embrace the viewpoint of another. As we strive to truly understand what others may perceive, and recognize the inherent limits of our own perspective, we allow ourselves to open up to new ways of being and a world of new experiences. And the more that we allow ourselves to truly embrace another's outlook, for all we can learn about ourselves and them, the more we are transformed by our sensitivity and are able to live with more empathy for one another.

Man is but one among millions of species of animals. What we hold in common is this planet that we share. But as we go about our lives, each of us does so from a different perspective. Even individuals among a given species—elephants, dolphins, dogs, cats, or humans—although they share similar features and forms, touch and see and hear the world through their own unique filters. The animals around us in our daily lives, from the hawk eyeing us from his perch high in the branches, to the smallest ant crossing our path as we step outside our door, can challenge us to stretch our perspective and inspire us to consider a world more lavish than we could ever grasp on our own—if we will only allow them to.

3
Mindfulness

When I lost my way, I was accustomed to throw the reins on his neck, and he always discovered places where I, with all my observation and boasted superior knowledge, could not.
—Napoléon Bonaparte about his horse Marengo

Dougal stretches out comfortably in the shadow of Andrea's chair, savoring the coolness of the exam room floor beneath him. With his rear legs sprawled out behind him, his massive frame extends the length of the picture window. I figure if he put his paws on my shoulders, he would stand close to seven feet tall. Though he lies just a few feet from me, I can barely make out his eyes behind the drooping locks from his forehead. He rests his head on his forepaws and sighs while I focus on the video. Yet, the constant shifting of his eyebrows and ears tell me he's watching and listening intently.

On the screen Dougal is standing in his living room. It is half past six in the morning and his family is in the midst of getting ready for work and school. In spite of the hour, he's fully alert, focused on one of the front windows—ears

pricked, as much as they can be for a wolfhound, jaw fixed
and slightly open, nose twitching in the direction of his gaze.
From off the screen, Andrea calls the kids to breakfast and a
string of children's voices passes just behind the camera.

Then a young boy appears in a corner of the screen. "Hey
there, Dougie. Here, boy! C'mon, it's time for breakfast."

Dougal licks his lips, turns to the boy, and then looks back
to the window.

A girl cries, "Eggs and bacon? Aw, Mommy, I thought we
were having waffles!"

A boy's voice chimes in, "Yeah, Mom. You promised!"

The boy walks up to his dog while Andrea reassures from
offscreen, "Don't worry. They're in the toaster. As soon as
you eat your eggs . . ."

Crouching to see Dougal eye to eye, the boy says quietly
in his ear, "C'mon, Dougie boy. Let's go eat. I'll share my
bacon with you!"

Dougal looks at the boy, licks his cheek, and, panting softly,
turns again to the window. The boy wraps his arms around
the dog's neck and buries his face in his mane.

From off the screen, a man's voice calls, "Billy . . . are you
downstairs? Your eggs are getting cold."

"Just a second, Daddy," the young boy answers, his voice
muffled by Dougal's wiry fur. He holds on, squeezing tight
with his arms. "Aw, Dougie," he says. Then he lets go, stands,
and runs somewhere behind the camera.

Dougal remains transfixed as if by something just outside
the window. Watching. Waiting. Unmoving. Then, all at
once, he pounces on the carpet just in front of him. His front

paws slap the floor and he points with his nose just above them, trapping some hapless insect as it skitters across the room. He lifts a paw, sniffs, pauses, then pounces once more on the rug ahead. Again and again, a few feet at a time, he tracks the course of his prey as it skillfully dashes across the floor. On the far side of the room, Dougal plants his feet on the wall, as the bug flees up toward the ceiling. Losing his quarry, he darts his head—first left then right—across the wall, and then again back down to the floor. Suddenly he freezes, turns his head toward the window, bounds back near his starting point, and resumes his chase again. For the next ten minutes, the video shows Dougal protecting his home from a bevy of insects as they slip inside, one by one, through the window.

While watching the video, I know from Dougal's history that the hunt for insects begins the same, without failure, every morning. It typically starts in the living room long before the family awakes, although later on, Dougie's search may lead him anywhere around the house. Tirelessly, he gives chase to any vermin that dare to enter their home until well into the evening. He takes his assignment seriously, dutifully standing guard throughout the day, aside from meals and playtimes. Even then, without encouragement from the family, he often skips breakfasts altogether and eats dinners only haltingly, while keeping an eye out for any pests. When outside the house, he lets go of all worries and relishes playing ball with the kids, but, back inside, he abandons all play and devotedly takes up his post once again.

The catch, of course, is that there are no insects. Flies,

gnats, mosquitoes, silverfish—the family's searches always come up empty.

More tellingly, should an ant or spider cross his path, Dougal rarely notices.

When the hunts first began, Andrea worried that fleas had overrun the house, despite Dougal's lack of scratching and the absence of telltale bites on anyone's arms or legs. Yet, a good bath and flea treatment had no effect on his behavior.

Just as the family began to wonder if the bugs might not be real, Billy solved the mystery one morning in the middle of getting ready for school. While the children sat around the breakfast table sleepily eating their cereal, Dougal chased ghosts nearby on the floor. A shimmer of light caught Billy's eye, and in a flash of genius, he got the idea that Dougal might be tracking his spoon's reflection as it bounced around the kitchen. Quickly, in a game of "let's try this!" all four kids discovered that forks, knives, cups, watches, buttons on their clothes, and backpack clips, if they caught a ray of sunlight, could send Dougal scurrying across the room.

The solution seemed simple enough to Andrea and William. So, after a family meeting and a round of sad faces from the kids, they resolved, just for one month, to separate Dougal during meals. The response was quick and quite dramatic. What once was a quirky habit at breakfast, within a week, had become a vocation. Dougal continued to chase reflections from watches to earrings, eyeglasses, and keys, but soon what began to inspire him most came from the headlights of passing cars.

Now, while the family sleeps, Dougal rises as early as three a.m. and stations himself on the living room rug, with a commanding view of all of the windows. There, in the darkness, he lies for hours—quietly, patiently, deliberately waiting. Those first beams of headlights from commuters on their way to work stir him into frenzied chases that last long after the kids leave for school. Likewise, the commute back home entertains him far into the evening until he finally collapses, exhausted, at bedtime. For Dougal, an innocent pastime has become an obsession, quite literally.

As I watch the video, the pattern is all too familiar to me: dogs chasing in all directions after hypothetical flies; viciously biting their own legs and feet until they are painfully bleeding and raw; barking for hours monotonously at unseen phantoms inhabiting the house; or drinking insatiably, and then peeing, inordinate amounts of water through the day. Amidst my files lies a fantastic collection of behaviors uncommon to the canine world. Of course, mannerisms such as these are certainly not limited to dogs. I've watched panthers pacing well-worn circles along the fence lines of their habitats; polar bears tediously rocking and weaving in front of their exhibit doors; zebras rubbing perpetually against the smoothened bark of live oak trees; and baboons methodically plucking their hair, leaving their bodies riddled with a patchwork of bald spots.

In my own family, our girl cat Clara ravenously seeks out and chews any plastics she can find—bags, straws, cables, speaker wires—along with a collection of other common household odds and ends. Mysteriously drawn to Crocs and flip-flops by some strange, supernatural attraction, she rav-

ages them with dozens of bite marks within seconds of dis-
covering them on the floor or in an open closet. All along,
while chewing, her eyes drift off into a faraway gaze.

Mannerisms such as these often fascinate casual observers. Knowing little or nothing about an animal's behavior,
they sense that they are watching something out of step with
nature. Yet I worry how often people make light of these
behaviors. Some figure these animals are bored and simply
amusing themselves in lieu of doing nothing. Others fancy
their habits as charming quirks to be captured on video and
filed away among the family's movies. Still others find them
delightfully funny, sharing them for the amusement and com-
ical relief of audiences.

When I look at these animals, though, I find something
entirely different. Instead of cute tricks, quirky habits, or
even mindless acts, I see animals suffering with an affliction,
in every sense of the word. Each is enduring emotional pain
that they are dealing with as best as they can. These rituals
develop purposefully to ease their very real distress.

As a veterinary behaviorist, one of my highest goals is
to ease my patients' suffering. To do so I must delve into the
inner workings of their lives to understand what drives their
behaviors—watching, listening, noticing, feeling. How did
the behavior first develop? When is it seen? What patterns
can I find? Does it vary from day to day or is it steadily constant? What happens just before each incident—with other
animals, people, and the environment around them? And
what about during and afterward? How do others respond

to their behavior? Are the animals themselves frustrated by their rituals or do the rituals clearly make them calmer?

Watching my patients with these questions in mind helps to guide me toward a diagnosis. For those with obsessive-compulsive disorder, I usually discover a telling pattern. I find most animals with OCD perform their rituals predictably— just before the keepers and trainers first arrive in the morning and, again, later in the day while the animals await their evening meal; when visitors cluster and crowd around the exhibit; as the family prepares to leave home each day for work and school; or while a neighboring tomcat tauntingly saunters by the living room window. Routine events of these animals' lives can actually add to their distress. Hour after hour they repeat their rituals in place of the pleasures they once enjoyed. Eating, playing, and even sleeping often suffer at the hands of their preoccupation. A young, healthy sheltie spins in circles rather than chasing and herding the kids in the yard. A golden retriever darts after shadows from tree to tree instead of tracking the fresh scent of a squirrel scrambling in the branches above him. Secretly nestled in a bedroom closet, a Burmese cat chews on wool sweaters until they are sopping wet and honeycombed with holes.

Few clients are surprised when I make a diagnosis of OCD. Certainly, some look at me in disbelief, hoping, instead, that I am speaking tongue-in-cheek about their animals' habits. Many more, however, seem almost relieved by my diagnosis. From movies and books, family and friends, and, in some cases, personal experience, they already know something of the quirky habits and mannerisms of humans afflicted with OCD. At some level they sense that their own hand washing, counting footsteps, and avoiding cracks in the sidewalk bear some resemblance to behaviors they have witnessed in their animals.

These rituals embody the compulsive element of OCD. Humans and animals develop these habits to contend with anxiety that riddles their lives. In fact, true to their diagnosis, they feel compelled to perform them. Day by day, practiced time after time, these patterns work as a coping mechanism, easing the stress that plagues their existence. Suppressing the urge to practice their rituals only worsens these individuals' angst. Yet, for all the attention we give these behaviors, they distract us from what is compelling them. If we could ask these animals, as we can with humans, what drives their compulsions, they would tell us of impulses, images, and ideas that very much have a life of their own. These obsessions, appearing to arise from nowhere, shatter every sense of normalcy in their lives.

What corner of the mind brings these obsessions into being? For that matter, from where do any of our thoughts emerge? What about our memories? Our hopes and dreams? Our fears? If, at a moment's notice, we can conjure an image at will, how is it that others slip into our thoughts against our steadfast wishes? How can a scent, drifting past us in a breeze, spark a faded memory, long forgotten from our childhood? How can glimpsing some obscure face from our distant past retrieve a swell of emotions, fresh and raw as if they were born just yesterday? In the middle of the night, as we toss between the sheets, what sparks into being the cryptic stories, spirits, and demons of our dreams?

Modern neuroscience offers us dazzling, true-to-life insights into the hidden inner workings of humans' and animals' brains. In the early 1950s, Wilder Penfield, a prominent Canadian neurosurgeon, laid the first stones in mapping out how our human brain functions. Desperate to remove a deadly tumor from the brain of his older sister, Ruth, and despite his belief that a physician should never "doctor" family members, he dared a radical surgery, attempted by few neurosurgeons in his era. By removing most of Ruth's frontal lobe, Wilder brought an end to her violent seizures, caused by the tumor edging its way through her brain. His groundbreaking surgery fully restored Ruth's quality of life for several years until, eventually, the tumor regrew and at long last overcame her. Taking umbrage at her death but, nonetheless, undaunted, Wilder devoted the rest of his life to helping other patients with neurological diseases.

For the next thirty years, Wilder Penfield performed surgery on more than seven hundred patients suffering from epilepsy. In the course of their treatment, each of these patients lay awake on the operating table numbed only by a local anesthetic, while Penfield's team of surgeons and nurses strove to pinpoint and remove the source of their seizures. After a barely imperceptible spark was discretely applied by a sterile probe to different regions of the brain, his patients described astonishing sights, sounds, and smells, as well as long forgotten memories, rushing forward in vivid detail. Meticulously noting each gyrus and sulcus (the mounds and grooves that blanket our brains), and diligently recording his findings through the years, Penfield plotted out the first working map depicting how our cerebral cortex functions.

Nowadays, doctors can reliably map the brain without ever cracking open our skulls. With sophisticated, noninvasive techniques such as magnetoencephalography (MEG), positron emission tomography (PET), and functional magnetic resonance imaging (fMRI), they can literally look inside our heads and watch our brains come to life in strikingly brilliant Technicolor.

Neurologists can now watch seizures in action, look for hallmarks of Alzheimer's disease, or trace where the blood vessels are strangled in stroke victims. Surgeons can dive deep below the surface of the brain to faithfully track down injuries, plot tumors, pinpoint lesions, and probe between the tissues well before they ever touch a scalpel to the skin.

These modern-day mapping tools reach beyond the realm of neurological disease to help patients with learning disabilities, behavioral disorders, and other conditions relating to brain function. Pediatric specialists can get a firsthand look at the brain activity of dyslexic children and predict with remarkable accuracy how well their reading will improve. Neurophysiologists can look at patients suffering from anxiety disorders to discover how their brains react to situations. Comparing neural pathways before and during therapy, doctors can measure how well their patients are responding to treatment. Shrinking their perspective to the size of a single red blood cell—smaller than the particles of dust floating past you as you read this page—researchers can now glimpse inside living animals' brains to study single neurons in action, as well as the corps of glial cells that dutifully nurse, feed, and support them.

With electrical impulses rippling in tiny waves along tens of thousands of branches, the neurons light up brilliantly as they relay their messages across the brain. Banding together in fiber tracts crisscrossing through the maze of cells, each of our brains' hundred billion neurons connects, on average, with more than seven thousand others. Each place where they meet, in waves of tiny droplets, a constantly changing tide of neurotransmitters ebbs back and forth between the cells. Ultimately, it is the give-and-take of these chemical messengers in our brains that triggers virtually everything we do, think, and feel.

As freshmen in veterinary school, we were taught that our brains were hardwired, and the window for change had essentially closed many years earlier. In spite of all our days spent scribbling notes in darkened lecture halls, late nights bent over lab tables while meticulously dissecting cadavers, and most other waking hours feverishly studying at our desks and cubbies, we learned that we were up against an inescapable fate. Facing the unavoidable death of thousands of neurons every day, the long-term prospects for holding on to all our newfound knowledge looked bleak.

More than two decades later, we now understand that our brains live in a state of flux, in which thousands of new neurons can be spurred into formation in a single day. Existing neurons sprout fresh branches to reach in new directions, framing and rewiring their synaptic links with other cells—new ones forming, others burning out. The simple act of learning stirs cells to strengthen their connections. These ties make it easier to send their messages and work as one. Their speed and efficiency become imprinted in their cellular memory, which, in turn, forms and shapes what we recall in our thoughts. This ability of the brain to endlessly refashion itself—what scientists refer to as neuroplasticity—allows us to adapt to ever-changing environments. As the world around us shifts and evolves, in a very real sense, so do our minds.

Observing routine human behavior as much as I do from day to day, I find it interesting how often society—from health insurers to our friends and neighbors—treats our minds and bodies as if they were separate. I cannot help but notice how we set apart mental illness from other diseases. It is easy to think of our neighbor stricken with cancer as a hapless victim. Yet, we may look at our colleague at work who's struggled through years of depression as somehow bearing a stigma.

This mind-set is no different toward animals. A cat disfigured with gnarled, crusty ears and scabby, cankered lips from pemphigus (a disfiguring disease in which the immune system decides to attack the body's own cells) is tenderly coddled by all in his family. Yet, another cat with a bald, bleeding tail who manically chases and gnaws it for hours is watched by her family with a certain reserve and, not infrequently, even disdain. Listening to my clients tales, I've noticed a common theme arises. People, by their nature, identify with their animals' behavior and often, in doing so, relate to it just as they would with fellow humans.

Certainly, we can influence what happens in our bodies but, all in all, we cannot direct our cells' and tissues' functions. To a large degree, they are governed by factors beyond our control: genetics, physiology, and the environment, to name a few. In health as well as disease, our cells follow their own destiny. Just as our hepatocytes can unwittingly go haywire, oozing streams of enzymes that run amuck inside our bellies, so can our neurons bungle how they communicate. When neurons and their connections malfunction, our senses, feelings, memories, and thoughts can wander, sometimes far off course.

In spite of all that we now know—or think we know—about our brains, we still have yet to understand so many fundamental questions. How does a bundle of cells give birth to thoughts and feelings? How do tiny waves of chemicals transform into a cherished memory? Why can a swell of emotions sway what we perceive and think? How can a cluster of neurons instinctively sense that we are in danger, in spite of everything that our eyes and ears may tell us?

The question of where our brain ends and where our mind begins remains as much a mystery to scientists as to peasants. The brain, of course, is made from matter: atoms and molecules that make up cells and the sea of chemicals within and around them. The mind, in contrast, is bodiless: a hazy, mysterious energy field made up of hopes and fears, thoughts and feelings, ideas and memories, wishes and dreams. How does matter manifest the abstract?

C. H. Vanderwolf, the esteemed neuroscientist, notes, "The conventional theory of the brain as the organ of the psyche or mind offers us the comforting illusion that we already understand the big picture."

It is naive to believe that the mind is nothing more than a cellular product. Without a doubt, our brain cells give rise to the energy fields of our minds. At the very same time, our thoughts, quite literally, mold and rewire our brain. Each unmistakably shapes and transforms the other.

As I make my rounds across the zoo, from The Tropics to Australasia, I must constantly bear in mind how the brain differs from species to species. The amount of space within the skull; the size of the centers for vision, smell, and hearing; the surface area of the cortex, including all the folds and grooves: Each reflects specializations in anatomy and function. These measurements tell me how each species has evolved and adapted from their perspective. When compared to the animals they hunt, carnivores have proportionally larger brains, presumably empowering them to craft strategies to catch their prey. Dogs have a pair of olfactory bulbs that, together, weigh four times those of humans, enabling them to smell secreted pheromones of fear from people. The area of the brain that integrates sounds is far more developed in dolphins than man, endowing them with the ability to know where they are and "see" by sound beneath the waves.

Although monkeys and moon bears surely differ, I am struck far more by their likenesses. From the thousands of synapses linking each neuron to the nuclei into which they cluster, the anatomy of our brains is remarkably similar from species to species. Even more striking to me are the likenesses between species' behaviors. Regardless of species, we rely on our neurons—second by second—for our very survival. From humans to apes and dingoes to dogs, we all use our brains to make sense of the world. Lights, sounds, smells, textures, and what we notice others doing are received, sorted, processed, and interwoven into a picture. We respond to this image with our instincts, emotions, thoughts, and actions.

Teaching is teaching and learning is learning, whether with chimps, raccoons, or beluga whales. And while I adapt my technique for each species, the principles stay constant. A wealth of brain research since those days of Wilder Penfield has granted us amazing insights into the inner workings of animals' minds. What these studies reveal, across a wide array of species, is that animals live intensely thoughtful lives. This research is affirmed every day in my work with patients. I have no doubt that animals' neurons are very much the same as ours, constantly generating images, emotions, memories, and thoughts—some trivial, others profound. Some animals, like Dougal, focus their thoughts obsessively; yet, their obsessions offer us a window into how they think. Though they may do so a bit differently from you or I, animals clearly perceive with awareness, think with reflection, and act with intention. As we do, they routinely take in their circumstances, as well as those of others, weigh their options, and consider consequences before deciding how they will respond. Doing so requires attentiveness, forethought, and consideration—all traits shared by humans as well as animals.

Surely, at times, animals act by knee-jerk reflexes, but then, of course, so do we. In my haste to prepare for dinner parties, holidays, and even family meals, I have burned

myself countless times while shuttling pots and pans across
the kitchen from stove to oven. Time after time, in my pain
and distress, I've acted impulsively on instinct: Cradling my
throbbing fingers, I've rushed to soak them in something
cool—flinging open the freezer drawer, scooping handfuls of
ice into a water-filled bowl while hastily scattering a dozen
other ice cubes across the kitchen floor, and bounding to the
sink to plunge my hand in the soothingly frigid water—all
the while yowling muffled cries of pain and disbelief. And
though I've resolved to pay better attention, I've still ended
up cooking recklessly. Over and over, in my shock and dismay, I've acted on impulse, with no more forethought than
a cat hissing and spitting from the prick of a routine vac-
cination.

Mindfulness is the state of being attentive in each moment to all that is happening within and around us. It calls us
to assume an observer's mind and notice our thoughts, feelings, and responses without judgment. Being mindful challenges us to be where we are with all our mind—unattached
to justifying or changing our experience.

An ancient Zen tale from Japan tells of a villager who is crossing a meadow when he begins to hear a rustling sound not
very far behind him. Stopping, turning, and scanning the
field, the man spies a pair of tiger's eyes—steadily, intently
staring in his direction. Startled and scared, especially out in
the open, he turns and flees, desperate to find somewhere—
anywhere—to hide. The tiger, in turn, springs from the grass,

giving chase and bounding through the field while the man, now panicking, runs as fast as his legs can carry him.

Finally reaching the end of the meadow, the man all at once freezes. Just ahead, no more than a foot away, the field ends in a perilous cliff. Beyond that and a hundred feet below, a river flows between the trees in a rocky, narrow canyon. Hearing the panting breath of the tiger closing in behind him, the man steps forward, sits, facing the dizzying height of the gully, and begins to slide down the rock wall. He figures anything is certainly better than a painful death at the jaws of a tiger.

Much to his amazement, after only a few yards, the man finds a gnarled, thickened vine growing from the craggy wall and into the ravine. Catching view of the tiger above him, he snatches the vine, wraps his legs around it, and begins to slide, inch by inch, lower into the gully.

With the tiger pacing back and forth a bit farther above him, the man breathes a sigh of relief and pauses to look down to the river gorge. Impossibly, far below, among the rocks where the vine lands, he spots another tiger lazily resting in the sun. The dangling vine, swaying back and forth, has clearly caught the second tiger's attention and, within a moment, their eyes meet. Too scared to go farther but too afraid to climb back up, the man decides to stay where he is, hoping that, with time and patience, one or both tigers will wander off. His feet find a small knot in the vine to help bear a bit of his weight, as he desperately clings with his arms and his legs.

As the man dangles in midair and wonders how long he

can hold on, he notices a scratching sound in the cliff face just above him. Looking up, he sees two mice—one black as night, the other a dusty white—crawling from a hole in the rocks. They scurry along a narrow path, and when they reach the vine they begin to gnaw it. Dismayed and dumbfounded as they chew away, the man realizes it will only be a matter of time before he falls to certain death.

At that moment, the man notices a small green bush growing from the rock wall. On a runner, a single wild strawberry grows, dangling, as he is, above the canyon. Carefully, gently swinging the vine through the air, clinging with one arm and stretching with the other, he reaches the berry with his fingertips and snatches it into his hand. With a tiger above, a tiger below, and two mice gnawing away on the vine, he sniffs the berry, places it between his lips, and takes a bite. Savoring its deliciousness, he realizes that never before in all of his days has a strawberry ever tasted so sweet.

When I first heard this story, I was touched by its symbols: one tiger, the past and how quickly we flee from it; the second tiger, our future and how we race toward it but also to our inevitable death; the vine, how tightly we cling to life as we know it; the two mice, day and night, mark the passing of time. But what I find most stirring is the strawberry's reminder to notice this moment and what is right in front of us, setting aside all our judgments, fears, and worries. Tasting the strawberry is the essence of mindfulness: embracing this moment for all that it offers.

The animals in my life model mindfulness in their simplest acts. At breakfast time, as we sit around the table, our

Labrador, Katie, rests on her bed just a few yards away. With each bite I take—even raising or lowering my fork—she is fully present, absorbed in the moment. As she looks our way, her nose twitches, catching the aroma of steaming scrambled eggs—nostrils flared, jaw lightly set, ears perked and tilted faintly forward, her eyes fix on any motion in proximity of my plate. I shift in my chair and cross my legs. Her eyes track me with impossible precision, noting every millimeter's movement in my body. A drop of saliva pools at her lips as she savors the fragrance of eggs from a molecule of steam that drifts across the room and floats into her nostrils. I have no doubt that just sniffing the eggs is as sweet to her as tasting the strawberry was for the villager.

In spite of all our human evolution, while our family sits at the table, laughing and sharing our plans for the day, I mindlessly filter out much of the moment. My stomach growling at the smell of fresh coffee. The delicious taste of hot scrambled eggs—the way they mingle with sprinkles of salt and almost melt when they touch my tongue. The warmth of the sun as it filters through the window. A cardinal diving down from the deck rail to snatch up a seed from the snow on our deck. The delight in my wife's eyes as she tells us a story. A missed look of confusion on my daughter's face. My growing concern, with the pace that we're eating, that the traffic will be heavy on our way to school. The tension in my voice as I dash out to the car. My self-judgment at the way I just spoke.

In our human condition we choose to ignore so much of what happens within and around us. We use the pace of our lives to excuse us from fully embracing what is happening now. Overwhelmed with input from others—gestures, expressions, intonations, spoken and unspoken words—we overlook a wealth of nuanced cues that deeply affect how connected we feel. Worried about past mistakes and stressed about the future—next month's bills, deadlines at work, and the meaning of the doctor's test results—we live much of our lives in regret and fear, running from one tiger and headlong toward another. And much of what we're yearning for, we are missing in this moment.

Turning to animals in our lives can inspire us to live more mindfully. Dogs, like Dougal in his obsession, and Katie in her incisive focus, point out to me a tiny piece of what I am missing at any moment. A dolphin lazily circles deep below me in her training tank; then, on the subtle prompt of a hand gesture from her trainer standing right by my side, she gathers speed, swims upward, and fluidly leaps through a ring dangled high in the air. Beyond her obvious intellect and talent, she reminds me to look more carefully for signals and cues from others around me. A bobcat's focus with every inch of his body on a gecko darting across a boulder prods me to stop and take in more sights, smells, sounds, and textures right before me that I am letting pass by. A Thompson's gazelle steadily gazing my way as she stands with all but her ears hidden in the grass—alert, listening, sniffing for any hint of danger or fear—stirs me to notice: What am I feeling *right now?*

Each animal's presence, through their example, suggests how I, in being more mindful, can make my life richer and fuller.

4
Responsiveness

*According to recognized aerotechnical tests,
the bumblebee cannot fly because of the shape
and weight of his body in relation to the total wing
area. But the bumblebee doesn't know
this, so he goes ahead and
flies anyway.*
—Igor Sikorsky

"How'd it go this morning?"

Sarah sighs and her eyes meet mine. "No trace of him yet—he's still inside." She turns back to the window and asks, "Did you take a look at the latest log?"

Tracing her gaze, I nod, "Last Thursday," and then continue, "What about since?"

"He came out quickly Saturday morning—same thing on Sunday. Gina was on." I hear it coming before she says it: "If I didn't know better, I'd think it was me."

I glance at her. "But, Sarah, you do." Her look is sober. Her cheeks are flushed.

I wait for a minute, but she says nothing, still watching the doorway vigilantly.

"Were you on Friday?"

"Uh-huh," she answers.

Pausing a beat, I then ask, "And?"

"Same as today . . . that's four out of seven."

I reach for my cell phone to scan the log. "Okay, that's this week. But, you know his charts. Two weeks before he shifted for you . . . twice. And the same—no, three times—the one before that. And, look, both weeks he wouldn't for Gina."

I turn to gaze at the plate-glass windows and the lush green habitat beyond. T'ika's no more than a foot away in a leaf pile just on the other side. Sniffing and pawing, she finds her target and—flash—in an instant it's in her jaws. She deftly totes it a few feet farther, away from the window where we stand, back to a clearing near the edge of the pond. Setting it down between her paws, she sits more comfortably camouflaged, her coat blending into the undergrowth.

And then I see him: a nose emerging within a shadow along the back wall—the doorway to holding (a set of rooms where both can rest while the keepers clean their habitat).

"A whole chicken today?"

"Mmm-hmm," Sarah answers.

"You crossing your fingers? It just might have worked."

She takes in a breath and says, "Yeah, maybe . . ." almost a question, with hope in her voice.

In the meanwhile, T'ika sits with her trophy, tearing the feathers out nip by nip and dropping them aimlessly at her feet. Those that cling to her teeth and muzzle don't manage to faze her, at least for now, as she plucks the chicken with practiced ease. Focused. Intent. Impeccably fastidious. The keepers' enrichment has served her well.

From the shadow behind her, a face appears. First muzzle and whiskers. Then eyes, ears, and neck.

"There you go, Yaku," I barely whisper, more to myself than anyone else. And then, to Sarah, "You got his interest."

"Well, yeah, but a chicken," she murmurs back.

And though I keep my eyes trained on Yaku, still I somehow sense Sarah's smile.

With nose and whiskers tugging him onward, he steps out farther while crouching low—ears pricked forward, eyes wide open. Then with a wince his ears flick back . . . and forward again. Hesitant. Furtive. Frozen—uncertain which way to go. He stands there midstep waiting for something. A clue? An omen? I can't say what.

We both stand with bated breath, still as stone, waiting.

I imagine I see resolve in his face, and then in a heartbeat he's by her side. And though I've studied them countless days—standing at these plate-glass windows, on my computer reviewing logs, or back at my desk poring through videos—together the two seem almost surreal. Apart from all I know of both and everything that endears them to me, I stand in this moment transfixed by their faces, the patterns of their spotted coats, which conceal them so effectively while they perch stealthily in the branches or on the ground between the leaves of their private jungle habitat, but also makes them appear at moments almost as if from nowhere by

magic—elusive whorls of red-gray circles outlined as islands
by bold, black rings, at places forming larger blotches or flowing hypnotically into streams. Captivating and mesmerizing.
No two cats exactly alike.

Of course, their brilliantly spotted fur was also the down-
fall of their kind. To make a luxurious ocelot coat it takes the
pelts of thirteen cats. But with a single fur coat fetching as
much as $40,000, hundreds of thousands of cats were hunted
each year, back at the height of the ocelot craze. Yes, that
was in the 1960s, although it maintained for twenty more
years, even with import laws in place protecting them since
'72. And their trading still continues, although more surreptitiously. Countless numbers of free-living ocelots lost to
nothing but human vanity.

Even aside from the fur trade of wild cats, man still poses
their greatest threats. Jaguars, pumas, eagles, and anacondas,
among a few choice predators, together barely rank fourth on
the list of what most often kills ocelots. The destruction of
their habitat (and ours), replacing forests with ranches and
farms, and being struck by passing cars account, respectively,
for second and third.

Though once they ranged much farther north to Arizona
and Arkansas, at most eighty remain in the United States
(half on private ranches and half on managed public lands)
and all in the southernmost tip of Texas. Even there, protected within the boundaries of a federal reserve, tourists in-
fringe as predators, striking ocelots with their cars—as many
as nine in a single year—in spite of posted caution signs glow-
ing brightly along the roads. So, though they once were quite

abundant, they now run the risk of becoming extinct and are listed as an endangered species—a testament to man's consumption and how well we care for our habitat.

Across the border in Mexico and beyond through South America, the picture is a bit more hopeful. Though numbers vary for different subspecies (distinguished in part by their locale but, more importantly, by their features), they're faring better than in the States. But the very same issues are taking their toll on a larger scale and at greater rates. And one more factor may be their undoing unless we step in to help their plight: Despite the fact that ocelots live throughout much of South America, their ranges have shrunk to rafts of land where once they were wide habitats. Within these man-made "islands" of cats, they're forced to intermingle and breed with all too dire consequences: loss of their diversity, less resistance to disease, fewer young conceived from breeding, and even less becoming adults. Right now as I write these pages, researchers and ecologists are struggling to develop a means to bridge together these stranded cats.

So, as with other endangered species, zoos end up playing a vital role in ensuring the future for ocelots. At the present time just over a hundred ocelots live in accredited zoos. And while in the wild the life span of ocelots is, on average, rarely more than ten years, in zoos they commonly live till twenty. Although zoos certainly can't match nature, endangered species can live in them sheltered from the risk of extinction and mounting threats they face in the wild. Watched over earnestly by their keepers and offered a rich environment, ocelots I've seen can thrive in zoos and safeguard the future

of their species while biologists, conservationists, park rang-
ers, and you and I strive to protect those remaining in nature.

If you took a tour of ocelot exhibits while traveling
through North America, you might be surprised by how
much they differ—in some a desert shrub habitat and others
a lush planted jungle scene. But this range of their homes
matches that found in nature. True to their felid lineage,
they've adapted well to diverse terrains—worlds apart in
many ways—reflecting their flexibility. In Laguna Atascosa,
their national wildlife refuge in Texas, beneath a skyline of
ebony trees and lonely, stargazing yucca stands, they live
in dense, sheltered, thorn scrub thickets. Yet, in South and
Central America they're found in much different environments: coastal marshes, mangrove swamps, grassy savannahs, second-growth woodlands, and beneath the rain forest
canopy.

"See that?" Sarah asks.

"Mmm-hmm."

"What just happened?" Yaku's stopped eating, though
T'ika continues, neatly tearing at chicken and bones and
swallowing both unchewed in gulps.

Yaku looks up toward the viewing windows but over a
bit to the side of us. I double-check, glancing over my shoulder, to see if perhaps there's someone approaching. At eight
o'clock, the path is still empty. He's noticed something—it's
not clear what.

*Did he see a reflection of light on the glass? Could he have
heard Gina humming a song while working with the tamarins?*

Did the howler monkeys' bellows grab his attention? An aracari purring? Zoo base on the radio?

He gives us a chance to see his face fully. Ears turned forward, eyes open wide, nostrils twitching, all senses aligned—his focus is riveted on the window and the path that lies beyond. But his pupils are dime slits, not wide-open circles. His breathing is easy. Muscles relaxed. It's clear to me he isn't scared. But something just distracted him. And then, again, he shifts his focus to somewhere just beyond the pond.

Tracing his gaze, I track where he's looking and spot something white in a nest on the ground. Squinting to view it better, I ask, "Eggs, too, huh? Are they whole or hollow?"

"Hollow," Sarah answers back.

"Catnip in them?"

"Mint and oregano."

Yaku sniffs the air and takes a step. We stand unmoving, watching him. Waiting to see if they'll pique his interest. If he'll crack them open. Rub and roll.

T'ika stops eating, matches his gaze, then stretches and walks off behind the pond. Yaku follows her path in step, a pace or two behind her tail. The veil of tangled vines enshrouds them, and both cats vanish between the fronds. Then T'ika, still leading, reappears through the ferns. She sniffs and considers, looks back toward their trail, then catches the scent of the eggs just ahead.

"Hmmm," I mumble. "Do you see Yaku?"

"No." I hear Sarah's voice is tense. "Do you?"

I peer through the leaves for a spot on his flanks. A hint

of black rings from a swish of his tail. Those long, sweeping stripes on each side of his muzzle. *No trace of him.* I scan the bushes again, watching for any hint of movement—a shift in the undergrowth, a wavering vine. *Still nothing at all.*

I answer, "No." But then I do. "There—in the tree, on that upper branch."

A nose and some whiskers rest on a paw. And above them, surreptitiously, two umber eyes gaze down steadily (almost imperceptible if not for the pale fur encircling them), their focus sharpened near where we stand—not quite at us but not far away. *Watching—or waiting—for something, but what?*

I turn to examine the trail once again, the viewing area where we stand, the rock wall, the window, the gardens around us. I listen for voices. I hold still for sounds. But still I find nothing.

Where is he focused? What is he hearing? What does he see that I somehow have missed? Can I really be clueless to what he is sensing after all the hours I've spent with him? And why does he linger there more days than not—or hidden in holding, refusing to leave—till well after closing and many times later, on into the evening, while T'ika roams their habitat indifferent to what imprisons him?

"I think that's it."

"Me too," I say.

"It's the same thing as always—just when I'm hopeful."

"I know." I turn to face Sarah again. *Oh, that look in her eyes—discouraged. Disheartened. One step from resigned.* I feel the same—but we won't give up.

"So, where do we go from here?" Sarah wonders.

I sigh. "I don't know what else to do."

She studies my face to take in what I'm saying, and then I continue, "Keep plugging away—reinforcing relaxed behaviors, target training, conditioning . . ."

"I know." She nods. "And he has improved. It's just that we . . ." Then her voice trails off.

"Want more for him," I say, completing her thought. With all the time we've worked together, we understand each other well. But, I feel somehow I have failed us all: myself, Sarah, Gina, T'ika, the zoo, but most of all Yaku, perched in that tree.

It's been two years since Yaku arrived as part of the ocelot SSP, the endangered Species Survival Plan, which links zoos together for ocelot breeding and helps oversee their care and well-being. As a male of Brazilian ancestry, Yaku was sent to be T'ika's companion and also with hope they'd eventually breed, helping to strengthen the gene pool of ocelots. The paperwork that came with him contained not only his pedigree but also a copy of his medical records as well as summary reports from the years at his former zoo. In short, he was a healthy, young male. No medical issues to speak of at all. No conflicts with Sumaq, his older companion with whom he'd lived for several years. And, though it stood in stark contrast to now, he'd adjusted well to the daily routine.

Yet, it seemed from the first day he came to this zoo, something was strangely amiss with Yaku. For seven full weeks he huddled in holding, refusing to leave by the light of day, though the keepers knew he'd slip out after nightfall from the scat they'd find in his habitat—on trails, in corners, and from time to time on logs—presumably left as a calling card to mark his domain with a comfortable scent.

When we look for ocelots living in nature, they're rarely, if ever, spotted by man, even those times that they hunt by day. For the most part, though, they're crepuscular (which means they're most active at dawn and dusk) as well as being nocturnal cats. In the dimness of twilight and darkness they roam, stealthily hunting large game and small prey in the cover of scrub thickets, jungle vines, and underbrush. And though they most often hunt mice, rats, and rabbits, ocelots catch small deer, monkeys, and birds with the same skill and cunning they stalk lizards and anteaters. Also being accomplished swimmers—a trait uncommonly found in most cats—those that live near rivers and swamps also often hunt fishes and crabs.

Although those in zoos live removed from nature, they keep the routine that they would in the wild, rising in the predawn hours until sometime around nine a.m. From then they lie low through the late afternoon, when they're once again active till sometime near ten. But none tend to be as reclusive as Yaku, resting hermitically all day long, withdrawn to the furthermost reaches of his habitat. Ignoring the routine of other zoo ocelots, he shuns most mealtimes, preferring instead to wait till much later—long after closing—to accept the remnants that T'ika has left.

Wild cats in zoos don't eat live prey for meals, unless an impetuous insect or frog just happens to stray onto an ill-fated path. For most zoos it's simply too expensive and impractical. But beyond these obvious justifications, I suspect the public would rather avoid the sober, unabashed realities of hunting—the method of killing, the struggle to live, the moment of death of another being, alive at one instant then gone in the next.

Indeed, those same truths confront us at mealtimes, whether eating at home or in restaurants, when we face the food on our own plates, but there it's detached from reality. When I watch others eat, I find it so curious how absently most people cut at their steak, tear off a chicken wing, or gnaw at a bone, without a thought about their prey, the abattoir, the life that passed. I don't believe it's done with intention. It's just that the meat is removed from its source—a fragment of another being. Having faced death from an early age—the slaughterhouse labs as an undergrad, vet school anatomy, clinical practice, and all my struggles through the years to save so many creatures' lives—where others see meat, I see flesh and bones. It's hard for me to divorce the two. But, then again, why should I want to, even if I somehow could?

If we set a mouse loose in an ocelot habitat, it would not be the same in the zoo as in nature—at least, I am certain, not for the mouse, trapped by four walls, unable to flee, its fate as fixed as a steer in a stockyard waiting for the inevitable. Perhaps it's too gruesome. It could be we're squeamish. Or maybe we just feel too vulnerable facing the death of another being and the fleeting impermanence of life itself.

So, zoos feed ocelots preprocessed meals: a commercial, precut felid diet with special meats added from time to time—turkey, venison, chicken, duck, rabbit. But since they don't hunt for their meals in zoos, they forage as an alternative. To meet this need—this natural drive to delve into their habitat—their keepers give zoo cats endless enrichment: chicken carcasses to pluck, tear, and eat; leaf piles to dig through and find hidden "gold"; banana leaf purses wrapped around turkey necks; frozen capelin floating in the pond; cowhides doused with antelope urine; pumpkins stuffed with cinnamon and clove; liver-laced ice chunks; eggs stashed in sand piles; catnip buried or sprinkled on logs. Devising these is never a goal; it's an ongoing process of learning what works. What sparks their interest? What brings them pleasure? What challenges them to think and invent? What brings to their lives a sense of fulfillment—replacing what's lost from the natural world with richness in their habitat? Sarah, Gina, and most keepers get this.

If we offer enrichment late in the morning or early in the afternoon, ocelots will adjust when they're active, despite their night-owl tendencies, and visitors will see an animate cat fully engrossed in his habitat instead of one passively sprawled on a log. But Yaku wasn't a typical cat. Those first two months he withdrew into holding from dawn to dusk habitually. Although it wasn't long after that—another month or two at most—he began to hide in the tree instead. Most mornings we'd find him aloft in its branches, but he still was reluctant to venture below except when the zoo was dark and quiet.

Then, one morning several months later, when Sarah arrived to begin her routine, she found Yaku peacefully lying with T'ika in a pile of leaves near the edge of the pond. To discover him there, we were stunned—ecstatic—though also confused about what could have changed. All morning, till T'ika retired to the bushes, he stayed by her side or not far away (not only when Sarah called both into holding, with chunks of fresh rabbit as their reward, but also when they were released again, once Gina had cleaned their habitat). That day he seemed lighter—more carefree, unfettered— heedless of what had tormented him, as if some ill omen had been removed, a demon vanquished, a spell undone. The next day, however, he'd returned to hiding, tucked in the tree till the keepers had gone and he could move freely once more by night's shadows.

Even so, from that point on, it was obvious Yaku had turned a corner. Though most mornings by far he still lurked deep in hiding, once in a blue moon he strayed to the ground before dawn broke over their habitat and stayed there through sunrise till late in the morning. Shadowing T'ika on those rare occasions, in the late afternoon he would follow her down and remain on the ground until well after closing. As fall led to winter, he did so more often. More telling to me, when he hid in the tree or hovered within the threshold to holding, I sensed in his features a conflict—his struggle to stay in seclusion or risk joining T'ika. Though he still showed no signs he was fearful or anxious, he preferred to avoid *it*—whatever *it* was—more days than not, roughly five out of seven.

So, as winter led to spring, we again explored his habitat and dissected every detail we could for what differed on good days and bad: the times they were fed; the climate and weather (temperature, humidity, barometric pressure, stormy days, cloudy days, windy days, rain, sun); sounds of neighboring animals; handymen, docents, keepers, and vets; zoo guests—their ages, numbers, behaviors; stray voltage from the lighting fixtures; the manner and means of their varied enrichment; the nuances of his bond with T'ika, both when they were together as well as when apart. Late nights at my desk I would stare at his image—probing his features, retracing his steps—as I reran his videos over and over. But at the end of the day, I was no more the wiser.

"Could Yaku be delusional?"

The question was posed by Dr. McCullough, a fellow clinician on the zoo's vet team. If we couldn't make sense from his life and routines of whatever it was that was bothering him, was it possible it could all be in his mind? Could Yaku be escaping from his own hallucinations—seeing, smelling, or hearing things that didn't exist in reality?

"Well, I can't say for sure, but I really don't think so. From all that I've seen of him, that doesn't fit."

Yaku's ease slipping down each night after closing; the way he'd relax when he was on the ground, roam through the ferns, dive into enrichment, stretch out with T'ika near the edge of the pond; and his calm, studied manner aloft in the branches, watchful and patient but never aroused— none of these fit with a delusional cat. But beyond any logic, I knew in my gut—by medical instinct or just intuition— that Yaku sensed something very real, to which he responded quite reasonably.

For a year and a half, like a dog with a bone, I gnawed at

the mystery of what bothered Yaku. Outside their window, I'd stand there and brood, lost to the world as I sorted it out. Yet, as much as I tried, I could not find a pattern. In spite of my searching, one didn't exist.

To be sure, though I sweated and stewed over Yaku, over time I admitted our prospects were bleak for solving the mind-boggling question we faced. So we focused instead on conditioning and learning—reinforcing those times when he was on the ground with jackpots of venison, turkey, or rabbit. With chicken in hand as a timely reward, Sarah helped shape Yaku's focus away from the window and toward his environment. Much to their pleasure he followed her cues and over time he did improve. Still, more days than not, he'd remain in the branches or linger in holding except after dusk, living only a trace of an ocelot's existence.

"It's getting late. I better go."

"Right," I answer distractedly.

"Where're you headed next?"

I check my phone.

"Cotton tops with Gina . . . then on to chimpanzees."

"Should I radio her that you're on your way?"

"Nah, that's okay. I'll stay here for a bit."

We say our good-byes and I turn to the window. With fragments of eggshells scattered around her, T'ika now sprawls near the ferns by the pond, leisurely gazing around their domain. I smile at the green flecks of mint and oregano loosely dusting her muzzle and cheeks.

Looking up to the branch where I last saw Yaku, there's not much to see of his face through the leaves: a beard of white that envelopes his whiskers; black freckles that splash down his muzzle and cheeks; the pink of his nose, just a dot at this distance. Our eyes meet each other's—a timeless instant, a glance of connection through windows and trees.

A pit in my stomach. Resolved to make his life better, all that I've done simply isn't enough. *Where do we go from here? What can we change for him? How can we bring more fulfillment to his life? What can I do to make a real difference?*

I search his eyes for a hint of an answer. He looks back at me with that calm, steady stare—patiently waiting for the menace to be gone so he can claim more of his ocelot's essence. Then he turns his gaze to the plate-glass window to resume his vigil of the path beyond.

In the eyes of a doctor, a patient responds when something about their condition changes as a result of the treatments we've offered or, in some cases, in spite of our care. Sometimes for the better and others for the worse, we look to our patients for signs of real progress—proof we're on target with our diagnoses, as well as on track in our treatments for them.

Though modern medicine is based in science, how we provide it is still much an art—a synthesis of our clinical skills: our bedside manner; how we relate to others; impressions, assessments, and decisions we make; the care and attention we bring to each patient. This is nowhere more true than in behavioral practice, where without the aid of definitive tests, we must strive to peek in our patients' minds—to grasp what they feel, understand what they're thinking—and then put in place a plan to care for them. How we respond to their state of being and they, in turn, respond to our care unfolds with the bond between doctor and patient. Yet, as much as our goal may be one and the same—to bring them comfort by some means of healing—our viewpoints will differ quite naturally.

Responsiveness is a quality of being by which we choose an action or feeling as a result of perceiving a stimulus either within or outside of ourselves. Distinct from reacting, which is mostly impulsive (and often results in some form of resistance), responding implicitly involves awareness. Responses imply introspection and forethought. Reactions, instead, arise instinctively. Responding is conscious, reacting reflexive. Both happen hand in hand, naturally—first instinct kicks in, then more mindful discretion—as a matter of course in both creatures and man.

From Yaku's reluctance to come out of seclusion, one might well believe that he failed to respond. Based on our efforts to change his environment, the months we invested conditioning him, and the countless hours we struggled and sweated, searching for why he remained so withdrawn, his progress in two years was hardly impressive. And yet, I'd assert he was highly responsive. Notwithstanding the plans that I'd laid out for Yaku, he chose to hide most days deliberately. In tune with his ocelot instincts and senses, Yaku perceived a discernible threat and mindfully heeded it with due discretion. And still, as he did so, we brooded and fretted, yearning to bring out a different response.

Consider an ocelot not in the zoo, reliant on keepers for

food and enrichment, but instead in the Andes of Ecuador. Nestled in the shadow of an active volcano and couched in a cluster of lush red-green bromeliads, she peers through the mist that bathes the cloud forest. An agouti, a few yards away, gnaws through the husk of a large brown fruit to get to the cache of Brazil nuts within, for the moment still oblivious to the peril lurking close at hand. Just as she crouches to spring toward her prey, the ocelot pauses a moment too long. Sensing some danger, the agouti looks up and, with no more than a breath's hesitation, scrambles toward the cover of his burrow down the slope.

In spite of a chance she could outrun her prey, she draws in her paws and squats closer to the ground. Ensconced in the mosses with leaves all around her, she furtively gazes through orchids and vines to the gnawed piece of fruit the agouti left behind. Though faint calls of songbirds are heard in the distance, the forest around her is quiet and still, as if nature had eerily fallen asleep. The moment is timeless and minutes pass by.

Then, without warning, the trees spring to life. With shrill chirps of alarm and a flutter of wings in a burst of bewildering yellows and blues, a bevy of hooded mountain tanagers takes flight. And from a limb just above where the Brazil nut fruit lies, a jaguar leaps down in a swift, blurry pounce, surveys his surroundings with penetrating eyes and, after several minutes more, ambles down the mountainside. Only then, with her role restored once again from prey back to predator, does the ocelot stealthily slip from her nest to resume her hunt by the fading light.

Hiding from a jaguar is without a doubt adaptive—for had she resolved to chase the agouti, she would, quite likely, have paid with her life. But what of our ocelots back at the zoo? Can we really be certain that Yaku's avoiding some harmless annoyance or unfounded threat? Or might it be possible T'ika's ignoring a very real hazard that Yaku has sensed? How do I, as a doctor, or you, an observer, with what we can see from our viewpoints as humans, judge the responsiveness of another being?

At times, I heard rumors of Yaku's mishandling when he was transported between the two zoos, as well as suggestions that, when he was younger, an uninformed keeper had mistreated him. Yet, as much as I tried to confirm these suspicions with past keepers, curators, interns, and vets, the best that they offered were just suppositions based on impressions they felt in their gut. I've seen where events, even several years later, in spite of the months without signs in between, all at once can induce an onslaught of symptoms. But, oftentimes, when I do find a history of trauma my patients have faced in their lives, my diagnoses remain much the same. In spite of the insight, more times than not, I still face the very same question: "Now what?" At that point what matters is how I respond.

The autumn of 1985 proved a turning point in my career as a vet, one that reached deep to my very essence, brought me to question my ethics and values, and has since imbued every part of my life: the tenderness I treasure as a father and husband; the connections I cherish with colleagues and friends; my empathy for others, both animals and humans; and the compassion that inspires so many choices I make. As I set down these thoughts nearly thirty years later, I remember that fall still so vividly.

We had just dipped our toes in the third year of vet school. With a wild-eyed excitement that had snowballed all summer—after two grueling years spent in lectures and labs in a torrent of formaldehyde, microscopes, and specimens—we were finally entrusted with our first chance in clinics. With stethoscopes draped round our necks, proudly worn as badges; manure-stained khaki overalls and blue scrub suits in hand; and student-length, white clinic coats (and in their pockets our bibles of notes as well as a small cache of instruments), we could now join the ranks of the upperclassmen to walk through the doors of the hallowed halls. Within those teaching hospital walls, though much of our duties took place late at night—checking on patients, meting out treatments, and scribbling our bleary-eyed notes in their charts, while still keeping up with a full day of classes—twice weekly we'd meet with real patients and clients while senior clinicians, their interns, and residents watched us and guided each step of the way. And though we'd only begun working with our first patients, it seemed what we learned in our classes each day took on a grand new relevance.

While spreading our wings as soon-to-be doctors meant taking on duties we'd dreamed of for years, it also led us into roles we'd dreaded. That fall we were plunged into one that was both: the realm of junior surgery. As freshmen we'd toiled in time-honored tradition through a formalin haze among well-preserved tissues, dissecting cadavers with meticulous care. At last it was time, as we started in clinics, to apply what we'd learned to real, living beings, before we stepped into the surgery suite. To do so, however, required we first work with dogs who had run out of time in a shelter.

As vet students, certainly, we were well versed in the daunting statistics of pets in this country: 70,000 dogs and cats born every day; 70 million living as strays; 6 to 8 million enter shelters every year, and well more than half of these tragically end up euthanized. Perhaps saddest of all, another 30 million more die every year of neglect, cruelty, and mishandling.

Knowing these cold, hard statistics is one thing, but facing them firsthand is quite something else. Putting a few of these dogs in our care on the day they were due to be euthanized forced us to take matters personally. For, in spite of our kindness and gentle attention, commitment and diligence in tending to them, sterile technique, leading-edge anesthetics, and a crackerjack team of clinicians at hand, in the end our procedures were terminal. Surgery—even when expertly done—once over is painful, takes time to heal, and can challenge both human and animal patients. So policy, ethics, and above all compassion dictated we would not cause them more pain than if they had been put to sleep at the shelter.

Each week in the morning, well before we'd begin, I could see our class buzzing with anticipation. This time it was us who were holding the scalpel, ligating the vessels, suturing skin, administering anesthesia, and tracking each vital sign.

Yet, prepared as we were from reviewing the textbooks—going over each step in the finest detail so once we were scrubbed in we knew them by heart—we felt the full weight and responsibility of caring for those creatures whose lives were in our hands.

At lunchtime while most of our classmates were eating and reviewing their surgery notes one last time, a few of us quietly slipped away to the kennel where the dogs stayed until lab began. Without many words but a look in our eyes that clearly expressed why we each were there, we opened the door and walked into the kennel to meet the dogs we would be working with soon—to take them for a walk; play with them on the lawn; let them sniff at a lamppost, the bushes, the trees; sit with them on the grass and do nothing together; pet them and hug them; let them know that we cared. At times in that hour, we'd catch a glimpse of each other and I saw in their faces what I'm sure was in mine: a respect for the lives of the dogs we were with.

That first afternoon, just before our procedures, while all of us scrubbed and got into our gowns, a few of our classmates asked why we came early, why we put ourselves through that ordeal. To be sure, it was painful, but also essential, the five of us felt, to go on with the surgery. And we did so each week for the rest of the quarter till junior surgery classes were done.

Times have changed quite a bit in the past twenty years. Notwithstanding the statistics of unwanted pets—the millions abandoned, abused, and euthanized—simulations and models now take the place of live animals for training vet students in surgery labs. I still think of those dogs, though, all these years later—the joy in their faces as we walked into the kennel; their simple abandon in our hour together; that soft, grateful look when their eyes would meet mine. And given what was required of us in that era of training, I could not help but choose to spend that hour with them.

We each must make choices of what we respond to. *In tune with his ocelot instincts and senses, Yaku perceived a discernible threat and mindfully heeded it with due discretion.* For even if a jaguar wasn't in a tree, who's to say his response did not serve him well, just because it was not what we wanted to see? How do we, as observers of other species, other human beings, people we know, judge the responsiveness of another being?

And still, as he did so, we brooded and fretted, yearning to bring out a different response. The animals I work with are in tune with their surroundings: other creatures, their environment, enrichment we may offer them, the cover that a tree or a holding room provides. All the while, we, as humans, struggle in our minds. *What should I do? Dare I act now? How will they react once they see my response? What if I think this out just a bit longer?* So, often we wait and postpone doing anything, choosing instead to avoid a response.

The question that I struggle with in caring about Yaku, the dogs in junior surgery, what food is on my plate is: *What can I do to make a real difference?* Creatures all around me remind me of that question in the choices they make on a day-to-day basis, the hardships they live with, the struggles they face, the fate they endure in our human hands, and the simple joys in which they celebrate.

The answer I hear, which they offer to all of us, is to trust in our instincts, wisdom, and judgment and risk doing something.

5
Expressivity

*Man himself cannot express love and humility by
external signs, so plainly as does a dog, when with
drooping ears, hanging lips, flexuous body, and
wagging tail, he meets his beloved master.*
—Charles Darwin

My favorite time to get to the zoo is just in time for sunrise, before the first of the keepers arrive, while the visitors to come that day are barely beginning to wake and stretch. I've always been an early riser, grateful for that sacred hour or two to be alone. At home, I mostly reflect and write while savoring the unruffled quiet, except sometimes for the scratch of footsteps from a chipmunk or mouse nestled in the attic. To sit in my office and sip on a cup of tea while the first rays of sunlight filter through the windows sets a pace to the morning that I carry with me through the day. All the same, to trade my desk for a frosted patch of ground at the zoo is even more beguiling.

The security guards at the gate recognize me, though I suppose they think me odd to arrive so eagerly and early.

Backpack slung over my shoulder with cameras and note-book tucked inside, I hike along the empty road that weaves its way around the exhibits. Today, I hop a split-rail fence and forge a path between the bushes to follow a hidden service trail. After climbing for less than a minute, I reach a shallow lookout and turn back toward the public viewpoint, level with where I'm standing, but a stretch away across a gully. Between us sprawls their habitat. I find the flattened mats of grass where I've sat on other mornings, shed my bag, unpack, and wait. The first hint of sunrise filters through the trees across the gully and dapples the ground with splashes of gold.

But for the waking calls of songbirds, the morning around me is still and silent. Most of the zoo's residents, though now awake, are still indoors, sheltered in their holding quarters to keep them safely through the night. Although I watch her step into the barn, no sound signals their keeper's arrival—not a scuffle of bodies from inside the walls, no bark or whimper before the door opens, not even the softened pad of paw steps. Nothing betrays that the three now roam freely—to reclaim the range of their habitat—except for a flash of fur in the trees. Phantoms in the woods. Elusive. Fleeting.

Although I blend well with the shadows sitting within the shade of a spruce, I sense that they are watching me. Even without a trace of fragrance from soaps, colognes, or other scents, their noses point to where I am sitting. In spite of my effort to stake them out secretly, without disturbing their morning routine, the tiniest sounds betray I am watching: the soft click of the camera shutter, the snap of a twig when I reach for my notebook, the rustle of pages as they flutter in the morning breeze. At home in the forest, instead of the zoo, they could hear an elk passing six miles away, and even farther if out on the open range.

I scan the edges of their enclosure, tracing a roughened, bare dirt path they've worn along the outer rim, without discerning a hint of movement. The snatches of the inner trails that I can see from above are lifeless. Nonetheless, I sense they're below me, hidden somewhere inside the thicket, exploring what's new since yesterday evening—a fallen tree limb knocked down by the winds, the scent from a rabbit grazing just before dawn, a fishsicle of ice left this morning by their keeper. Yet, from what I can see of them from where I sit, they're as good as ghosts. But then I hear their distinctive howls—first the male, Kaskae, deep, resonant, and bold, then Kesuk and Neka, higher pitched and more melodic. Even in the light of day, I feel a primal instinct stir.

Humans' fascination with wolves predates our existence as a species. Long before the caves of Chauvet and even before our forerunners were human, reaching back half a million years, skeletons of *Homo erectus pekinensis*, more well known as Peking man, have been found intermingled with those of prehistoric wolves, suggesting that, at times, they likely shared a common shelter. Before they ever reached that point, they watched each other from a distance. And we still do to this day. When hiking in the wilderness, we find their paw prints crossing our paths. From time to time, in woodlands and pastures, we spot the remnants of their prey. Comfortably settled inside our cabins, we hear their howls from the darkness around us—sometimes a lonely voice answered only by a distant echo and other times an eerie choir, chanting in the black of night.

A trapper once described the howl: "Take a dozen railroad whistles, braid them together, and let one strand after another drop off, the last peal so frightfully piercing as to go through your very heart and soul."

The wolf's howl both haunts and enchants us. It conjures images of mystery and menace, of kindred spirits and beasts lurking in the shadows biding their time, waiting to devour us, more aware of us than we can ever be of them.

Although there's no truth to the story, some imagine that wolves howl to the moon, inspired, perhaps, by some mystical urge. For wolves, however, their howl has meaning. Sung in solo or joined in chorus, they howl not only on moonlit nights but also at new moons, dawn, twilight, and, now and again, during the day. While apart on their nightly hunt— lone wolves treading for miles through the forest or scouting across the open range—they stop to howl to keep in touch as well as to gather the pack together to rendezvous, to chase for prey, and, when they are done, to return to the den. Where the pack's terrain runs close to that of other wolves, a group howl can ward off outsiders, avoiding the risk of a confrontation as well as protecting a recent kill. Two wolves howling together, varying in pitch and tone and echoing off the walls of a canyon, can easily sound like many more, daunting even the bravest of strangers.

To those in the group, though, howling works as a sort of glue, helping to strengthen the bonds they share. But wolves connect with more than just howls. Scientists sort their

vocalizations into squeaks, whimpers, barks, and growls; however, in truth, these are man-made abstractions. Wolves
speak in a spectrum of voices in order to relate with one another. Squeaking, for instance, a high-pitched sound offered
when close to other wolves, can be expressed in many ways—
softly, loudly, cut short, or drawn out—to take on different
meanings in play, in greetings, or when a wolf is anxious.
Each distinct utterance conveys to others a different intention, somewhat as does language for humans. But unlike our
human words, wolves' sounds lack precise definitions. Their
timbre, tenor, duration, and pitch, the context of what is
happening at that moment, and the details of their relationships can change the meaning of their message. And sounds
form only part of the picture.

Despite their nuanced use of voices, wolves rely on their
other senses at least as much to communicate. Often without a single sound, wolves relate in a ballet of movements
blended with postures and facial expressions to convey what
they think and feel. A twist of an ear, an indirect gaze, turning aside in another direction, a raised paw, a chin on a
shoulder, a brief flash of white in the eye, a tentative lick of
another's muzzle—each subtle gesture is telling, but joined
together they are filled with meaning.

As they finish their morning howl, Kesuk and Neka head
into the open and, after a few inquisitive sniffs, start to lick
at the block of ice. Kaskae follows them into the clearing,
approaches the pair, and lingers a moment—tail extended
straight with his back, ears and whiskers fully turned forward,
focused on Neka crouched just beneath him. He angles his

chin just above her shoulders, suspended an inch or two in midair. Young Neka shifts in less than an instant and leans away from the elder wolf. She tilts her head, flattens her ears, subtly tucks her tail a bit tighter, and stretches back the corners of her lips to bare her upper row of teeth. What I see as a deferring grin many mistake as overt aggression.

Even among trained observers—graduate students studying wolves day in and day out in the field for months—it's easy to misinterpret signals. A snarl of teeth, a grimace, a growl—each cue by itself means little, when dissected, analyzed, and annotated apart from the moment. In human language, a single word can be defined in many ways until we join it along with others and link them together to form a phrase. In a flash, our manner of speaking, a nuanced inflection, our choice in words infuse our sentences with meaning. Despite the linear flow of prose, we express our thoughts in a world of dimensions. In their own language, likewise do wolves.

The wolf pack is a tightly knit group mostly made up of a nuclear family: a father, mother, young and old pups, and, in certain instances, others. The idea that wolves come together—a disparate league of loners and rogues—to form a band simply isn't true. Instead, much as in human families, the ties between wolves are close and strong with parents assuming the leading roles. Contrary to popular myth, there is no alpha wolf in nature. This outdated notion is coined from old research based on studying captive wolves grouped by humans—instead of by their instincts—and forced to live with one another. Nowadays, the concept of an alpha wolf is obsolete. Wolves in a pack don't rule by conquest, directing others by will and force. Instead they lead inherently as parents, guiding the pack with confidence and, when needed, correcting with directions, not unlike what we aspire to do in human families. Evolution favors the wolf who focuses on what matters most: finding food, remaining healthy, resting, breeding, caring for young—not confronting and dominating others. The same is true for every species.

The dominant alpha never existed—neither did his subordinates—except in the minds of human observers imposing structure upon the pack. No wolf rules supreme until he dies or is weak and feeble. Instead, wolves assert, defer, and cooperate with one another, negotiating their relative roles situation by situation. Though no doubt the parents lead, everything is contextual. Overt conflicts do occur, but not nearly as much as most people believe. Often, signals shared by wolves observers mistakenly view as aggression. Yet, in wolf language, they are crucial displays, ripe with feeling, intention, and meaning.

Together with dingoes, dogs and wolves comprise the members of *Canis lupus*. Though all belong to a single species, each remains discretely unique. Circumnavigating the globe, wolves diverge into many subspecies—thirty-seven to be exact—each discernible from the others. Because of widespread obliteration across much of their natural range, many of these are now extinct, or their status is listed as "unknown" (which means one hasn't been seen for years). Within the survivors that do remain, most are endangered; a few are not. Although we can distinguish each by genetics, features, or habitat, behaviorally they all are the same. Mexican, Arctic, or Eastern wolf—why they howl, how they lead, what they convey in their postures and signals endure unchanged between subspecies.

From Newfoundlands to Lhasa apsos, despite the amazing array of breeds, all dogs belong to a single subspecies, *Canis lupus familiaris*. And yet, they are distinctly different. Intrinsic with their domestication over the past millennia, humans bred dogs for different traits—aptitudes, skills, appearances—all to suit our wishes and needs. Along with favoring physical features—massive bones for hauling and pulling; long, sleek bodies to chase after prey; strong jaws and short legs to ferret out vermin—we've also bred for specific behaviors, often by intention but other times without a clue. Once essentially nonexistent among a number of popular breeds—Bernese mountain dogs, golden retrievers, and Labradors, to name a few—aggression is now more prevalent among the canine cases I see. Obsessive-compulsive disorder afflicts more dogs in certain breeds, causing Doberman pinschers to suck at their flanks, German shepherds to chase their tails, and miniature schnauzers to stare at their rears. At times we've been so focused on selecting dogs for certain traits that we've unwittingly let others slip by us, sometimes unnoticed for generations.

From man's contrivance through the years, the traits we've chosen for each breed add a twist to how they express themselves. A boxer's idea of wagging with glee—his full rump wiggling side to side—is different from that of an Irish setter, broadly sweeping her feathered tail. A Sheltie eager to go outdoors spins in circles and barks in fits; beside her a Newfoundland licks his lips, pants, and soaks his bib with drool, while gazing longingly out the door. No wonder they look at each other befuddled and end up misreading the other's cues. Comparably, wolves have it easy.

Wolves live in packs, but dogs do not. Even in groups of feral dogs, what keeps them together is different from wolves. Among those dogs without a home, living by their own devices in cities or the countryside, they band together to defend by numbers—to protect their food and territory from other dogs, wild canids, and scavengers of other species. But without abiding family ties, hunting, breeding, and caring for young are not supported by the group. They lack the cohesiveness found with wolves. Without the intimate bonds of the pack, how well they relate to each other suffers. Not sharing the depth of connection of wolves, they depend even more on how they use signals. And therein lies a challenge. Their differences in body shapes, aptitudes, and temperaments affect how they communicate—how well they move, their tone of voice, the ways they respond to one another. Some disparities are obvious, but many more are unobtrusive, even to a skilled observer.

With over five hundred breeds of dogs that have been contrived and bred by man, I find it truly remarkable that so many relate as well as they do in most conditions and situations. Without the structure of the pack, and often at the end of a leash, to be controlled at people's whims, most dogs manage to signal each other and interact surprisingly well. Even when they are set free to roam at the park or in the country, they somehow seem to overlook or allow for all their differences. Yet, among all the files that line my shelves lie the exceptions in which they do not. Such is the substance of interdog conflict, human-directed aggression, and more.

Most dogs, such as Murray, express themselves quite capably, regardless of their body shape, character, or temperament. I've come to visit him this evening along with Kim and Michelle, his owners, to see how well he has improved at playing in the dog park. Three months ago, when I last saw them, Murray had lingered near the fence, refusing to look at other dogs, or closely clung to Kim and Michelle, eyeing them for any clue that they were ready to head back home. At barely twenty-four inches tall and weighing somewhere near seventy pounds, he's roughly average in height and weight compared with the other dogs today, the smallest being a papillon and the largest a Scottish deerhound. Two other Labs—one chocolate, one black—pull at opposite ends of a stick, stubbornly growling and wagging their tails. Murray watches a few steps away, his buff-yellow coat highlighting his features: eyes squinted; eyebrows shifting; tail wagging haltingly; hackles smooth—raised—then smooth again. He studies the tug-of-war for stretches, but stops at moments to look away. Everything about his manner signals his ambivalence, a marked improvement from his earlier fear. Although he finds their play attractive, together his features convey his doubt. He hovers near, but he's uncertain whether or not he'd like to join in, what to do, or how to do so, and he clearly expresses this.

A large dog—I can't make out the breed . . . perhaps a terrier-mastiff cross—just off-leash rushes up to Murray. With the stranger standing a half foot taller, directly in front of him nose to nose, Murray understandably freezes. His eyes avoid the other's stare. He raises his hackles and drops his tail, tucking it lower between his legs, unwagging except for a trace at the tip. The stranger steps forward now cheek to cheek and boldly sniffs at Murray's ears. Standing several yards away, I still see Murray's body tense. He crouches slightly, leans away, pulls his upper lip back in a grimace, and flashes his teeth in a nervous smile. Although the setting and actors differ, I think back to Neka deferring to Kaskae. All the while, the other Labs continued earnestly at their game, oblivious to—or ignoring—the stranger.

Murray chances a step away, and the larger dog shifts to sniffing his rear. In turn, Murray stands still as stone—head low, shoulders rigid, no trace of a waver in his tail. Only his eyebrows dare to move, first darting one way and then another. A nervous drool builds at his lips and begins to dribble down to his chin.

Instincts heightened to full alert, I turn to look for the stranger's owner and see him frantically running our way shouting, "Kafka, no! Get over here. Now!"

A sudden yelp, deep bark, and growl jerk my attention back to the pair. The larger dog now towers over Murray, forepaws squarely on his back, sounding a menacing, guttural growl. In our rush to intervene, Kafka's owner, Michelle, and I converge upon the pair as one. Kim arrives a moment behind us.

In an instant with stunning speed, the owner snatches Kafka's collar and swiftly wrenches him off Murray with such proficiency I'm certain he has practiced this before. After a terse apology, with Kafka now solidly clipped to a leash, he hurriedly tugs his dog away, across the pen and out the park gate.

As I look Murray over for wounds, I hear Kafka's owner scolding from a distance, "Listen to me! That's it—we're leaving. I've had enough of you today."

Although I missed the instant when Kafka jumped on Murray's back, it's safe to say that Kafka's response did not match up with Murray's cues.

From watching Murray's signals with Kafka as well as with the other dogs, I'm certain he clearly expressed his intentions. On that evening, as other days, Murray signaled his deference. In contrast, Kafka asserted himself to the point of ignoring Murray's cues, possibly by choice or perhaps because he did not recognize them.

The manner in which puppies are raised, how and when they're socialized, their experiences while growing up as well as when they are adults, their genetics, and their personalities (the essence that makes each dog unique) all factor into determining how dogs relate and respond to one another. The same can be said for all other species, humans as well as animals. How each of us relates to others is intrinsically based on who we are: our essential nature or character, experience, and disposition. It shouldn't be surprising, then, how two different individuals, both in the very same situation, can respond in entirely different ways. Likewise, when we reach out to others, as we convey what we think and feel, who we are inherently affects how we express ourselves.

The very act of communicating depends upon two separate beings: a signaler, who sends a message, and a receiver, who perceives it. Setting aside the message itself, whenever we act as a signaler, what and how we communicate relies upon three crucial factors: how well we convey ourselves (what are we thinking, intending, and feeling); by what means we are sending our message (sight, sound, touch, smell, or perhaps some extrasensory means); and how the other perceives our message (how well they comprehend what we wish to convey to them).

Expressivity is a quality of being that reflects how well we convey our thoughts and feelings. Murray and Neka express themselves through an eloquent repertoire of signals—gestures, postures, facial expressions, manners of touch, vocalizations, and even secretions from glands in their skin. Mingled together to form a picture, these signals clearly portray to others what they are thinking, intending, and feeling. Though Kaskae responded in a way that made sense for the message received and Kafka did not, Neka and Murray both conveyed themselves expressively.

When humans communicate with others, most often we think of relying on words. As I sit now and write these pages, I often spend hours reflecting on words—which ones to use and how to arrange them so I can best be understood.

Poets, playwrights, lyricists, authors all rely on written words to convey their message in place of signals. Yet, beyond the written page, words, of course, can be spoken and heard—shouted loudly, whined, shrieked, moaned, or whispered in confidence, softly into another's ear—all with an array of intonations and inflections. Even as we talk together, informally and one to one, we often try to pick and choose the words we use to best portray our inner thoughts and feelings.

Through our human use of words, we distinguish ourselves from animals. Woven together in intricate ways, words represent a world of symbols, as meaningful to us as Murray's signals are to him. But though our language—spoken and written—is inextricably part of us, it also can be our Achilles heel. The English poet laureate Alfred, Lord Tennyson once wrote:

> For words, like Nature, half reveal
> And half conceal the Soul within.

We focus so much on what we say, putting stock in our choice of words, that we often fail to pay attention to all the many other ways that we portray our inner world. Just like other animals, we convey what we feel by unspoken signals.

Our facial expressions; how we stand; which direction we look when we're speaking—a glance away, a brief look downward—our eyes opened fully, squinting, or closed; the movements and gestures we make with our bodies—arms stretched wide, reaching out for a hug, or folded together across our chest—our depth of breath and the rate we are breathing; and even our secretion of pheromones, released and wafting through the air—all convey our feelings to others, whether noticed with awareness or registered without a thought.

Extensive research with human beings clearly notes and underscores how much of what we relate to others occurs outside of language and words. And while we often must sift through phrases in order to grasp what another intends, we pick up on nonverbal cues in an instant. Even when words disguise others' feelings, we notice these signals instinctively. Yet, though the essence of this research is common knowledge in modern times, we continue to focus mostly on words when expressing ourselves in our day-to-day lives. We talk to family, friends, and strangers most of the time oblivious to, or at least ignoring heedlessly, all that our other signals reveal of us.

For all our emphasis on words and the beauty and detail that they can convey, in using them to express ourselves, we often fail to take the time to relate well what we are feeling. Particularly with written notes, scribbled hurriedly onto a page or hastily entered into a keyboard and sent by email with only a click, sometimes without a second thought, we offer little else to interpret except for the literal meaning of the words. Without our cues in intonation, expressions, gestures, or manners of touch, it's easy to send a misleading message and easier yet to be misunderstood. Even watching people speaking in conversations one-on-one, far too often I see them talking on and on without a pause; their words say one thing, their bodies another, and all they want is to be understood.

In the frigid waters of the North Pacific, somewhere far offshore between the Aleutian Islands and California, a single whale swims by himself away from others of his kind. The course he travels differs from the migration routes of other whales, and it varies widely from year to year, mostly tracking a north-south axis but sometimes heading far out west, reaching toward the mid-Pacific. Other times his route seems aimless, a random series of lines on a map.

Although no human has ever seen him, scientists have tracked his movements for years through an extensive array of hydrophones first set up by the U.S. Navy to listen for Soviet submarines at the height of the Cold War. What sets this whale apart from others and allows his path to be traced at all is the distinctive stream of sounds he makes as he roams beneath the waves. Presumably, he's a baleen whale (a filter feeder, lacking teeth) because of the nature of his calls.

Toothed whales (or *Odontocetes*)—such as porpoises, dolphins, and beluga whales—produce a range of high-frequency clicks that help them forage and navigate as well as to communicate. Baleen whales (or *Mysticetes*)—such as blue, fin, and humpback whales—in contrast, create low-frequency sounds, some below our human range of hearing, it's believed for social reasons—courting, mating, caring for young, and connecting with others in the pod—but also, perhaps, for navigation.

Most of the baleen whales in these waters sing near 15 to 25 hertz, except for the well-known humpback whale, which reaches vastly higher notes. The song of this solo whale, however, hovers near roughly 52 hertz—in the low range of a contrabassoon or tuba—unlike that of any known whale. Although no one can even be certain, most scientists believe that he's a male and his songs are his searching for a mate.

The researchers who've studied him most have suggested a number of theories for why this whale's song is unique. Most likely he suffers a deformation, which probably happened before his birth, that affects the patterns and notes of his songs. It's possible that he's the first of his kind—the unique offspring of an unlikely mating of blue and fin or humpback whales. Or, although it's considered unlikely, perhaps this whale is the last survivor of some long-lost cetacean species. Whatever the cause, he swims alone, wandering through the vastness of the ocean and singing songs that go unanswered.

Dubbed the "52 hertz whale," he caught the attention of scientists after he was first identified and noted in an obscure report. Then, after being tracked for years with a research study devoted just to him, he captured the imagination of the greater public after Andrew Revkin wrote about him in the story "Song of the Sea, a Capella and Unanswered," which was published in the *New York Times*. And through the years, from reports in papers, podcasts, blogs, and dinner conversations, he's continued to touch people's hearts and minds.

I believe it's more than coincidence that a whale who cannot connect with others of his kind can so profoundly speak to us as humans. Though few of us have heard his calls, his message somehow reaches us. Among those who have heard his voice, none can begin to fathom the meaning of the moans, clicks, purrs, and trills of his songs. Of course, we lack a whale's perspective: his underwater view of the world, shaded in hues of green and blue fading deeper into the darkness; the otherworldly landscape of oceanic rifts, canyons, and plateaus; the array of creatures swimming beside him and the spectrum of sounds that they create, surging for miles beneath the waves, enveloping him and passing on. But beyond their foreign land and language, whales relate with a different awareness than we do as human beings.

The animals right within our grasp—the dogs and cats in our own homes, the foxes and deer that roam around us, the wolves and elephants at the zoo—can speak to us as effectively as one lonesome, singing whale endlessly searching for another with whom he can communicate. Instead of running on automatic, relying on words to convey to others everything we think and feel, the animals right by our side can remind us of the other ways we can express ourselves—and, truth be told, already do. But first we must be willing to notice, take stock, and be accountable for all the messages we relate, spoken and unspoken.

Our ability to express ourselves—to be seen, heard, and understood; to connect with others, as we long to do—depends upon us fully claiming all the ways we communicate. As we accept how we convey our thoughts and feelings beyond words we use—through the tone, pitch, and pace of our voice as we speak; our postures, gestures, and facial expressions; the ways we look into another's eyes (or don't)—we more fully relate to those in our lives. And as we communicate with clear intention, while being mindful and sensitive, we more fully embrace our human nature.

6
Adaptability

Everyone thinks of changing humanity, but no one thinks of changing himself.
—Leo Tolstoy

Baxter never really was a city cat. But life with Jen in the woods of Lake Tahoe was, still, quite different from living in Arcadia, California. First of all, back when Jen was a student, most days she spent much of her time away from home. Then there were the roommates, Carrie and Alexa; a constant stream of friends dropping by throughout the day; a decent amount of space to wander; and though there were no other cats in the house, Carrie's bulldog, Bandit, could be a pest when he got excited. But the biggest difference between then and now was before he had a cat door to come and go as he pleased—to explore the yard, roam through the neighborhood, or hunt for chipmunks and birds in the woods—and now he was an indoor cat. Still, even then, back at their old house, when Jen was not at classes or work, Baxter's favorite place was by her side.

As Jen explained to her sister on the phone the other

night, "I'm sorry, Julie, it's not worth the chance. This is the
real forest, not the old woods back where we lived in Arcadia. He could wander for miles—he could get lost . . . and
even if Bax did find his way home, there're all sorts of animals
out there—I mean serious ones like bobcats, and coyotes, and
cougars, and bears. They really could hurt him, even *eat* him."

"Cougars."

"Well . . . maybe not *cougars*."

"Jen. It's not like you're living in the Yukon wilderness
or—"

"No, Jules, really. He'd just, like, vanish and I'd never . . .
even know."

"Okay already, I hear you, Jen. It was just an idea . . ."

And still as the discussion changed to jobs and dating,
Baxter cozily stretched in Jen's lap, while they gazed out into
the darkness together.

With only just the two of them, their cabin in the woods
was much roomier than they were used to: two bedrooms,
two bathrooms (one converted to a darkroom), a small loft—
one of their favorite spots—which they reached by climbing
a spiral staircase, plenty of closets, and the great room, where
the kitchen and living room looked out through picture windows to the thick stand of forest that lay just beyond. There
was also a deck on the back of the cabin, from which you
could barely make out through the pines the North Shore
of Tahoe and Carnelian Bay. The second week in their new
home, before the chill of fall set in, Jen wrapped chicken wire
around the sides of the deck to give Baxter a place he could
go outdoors, just to be in the open air. With the steep slope of

the mountainside a good twenty feet below, he seemed content to have the space and never tried to climb the fence
or the trees just on the other side. In fact, while Jen worked
in the darkroom on her photos, the odds were, when she
stepped out for a break, she'd find Baxter sunning on the deck
or, if not there, dozing up in the loft.

As fall gave way to winter, though, and the thick Sierra
snowpack grew deeper, Baxter discreetly avoided the deck
except when Jen would coax him out with his favorite freeze-
dried salmon treats. Even then, when the treats were gone, he
would spring from Jen's lap and run across the deck and back
inside through the sliding doors to the warmth and comfort
of the cabin. Every few steps, he'd stop and shake the snow
from his paws with a look of disgust and, once back indoors,
he would curl up on the rug and lick at the fur between each
toe until the very last snowflake had melted.

Jen wasn't really certain exactly when Baxter's "fits" first
started. "I think it was maybe like . . . two or three months
ago, 'cause it started snowing in the middle of October . . .
and it wasn't too long after that, I remember him doing it."

The bouts in the beginning were so brief—a few
seconds—that, at first, Jen thought he was just twitching his
tail. As winter set in, though, she noticed the episodes more
and more often and lasting much longer.

In a video Jen took of one of his fits, I watch Baxter scramble frantically down the staircase and dash across the kitchen
floor, heading toward the bedrooms. About halfway there he
freezes, turns, stares at his tail for several seconds, and then
takes a few halting steps. All of a sudden, he turns toward

his rump and begins to nibble it furiously. After a minute, he finally stops and looks around the kitchen with a vague, distracted gaze. His tail twitches several times and I notice him pant as he turns toward the camera. He takes a step, hesitates, and then charges full speed across the room, almost as if he were being chased. As soon as he comes within reach of the sofa, he leaps onto the cushions and burrows deep into a corner, a tiger lurking furtively within the shadows of his cave. The only trace I see of him is the tip of his tail between two pillows.

"When did you begin to notice episodes like this one?" I ask, looking back from the video to Jen.

"Maybe, at first, once or twice a week, but now he can have two or three in a day."

"Is there a time they're more likely to happen?"

"Not really. I've tried to figure out a pattern—even plotted them on a chart—and they just don't seem to make sense to me."

We look at the chart in his file together.

"One thing I should say, though," Jen continues, "is that I've only seen them during the day."

Looking up from the chart, I ask, "*None* at night?"

"Well, maybe he has some while I'm at the café, but I've never seen one on my nights off, either. Don't you think that's kinda weird?

"And once we're in bed for the night, Bax loves to snuggle in the covers till it's morning. So, I'm sure I'd wake up if he had any then."

From the rest of Baxter's history, he appears to be a

normal cat. He's social with friends, very affectionate with Jen, eats by grazing on and off throughout the day, and loves to play any time she's willing.

"His favorite game, by far, is fetch. You really need to see this," Jen says, as she crumples a sheet of paper and wads it up into a smallish ball. Baxter's ears perk and his eyes open wide—fully alert, though he doesn't move a muscle. Jen tosses the ball and his eyes track it with flawless precision as it arcs through the air, lands, and rolls across the floor. When it finally stops, he stares at it, transfixed and frozen; then, all at once, he vaults from his resting place beside me and, within a few bounds, lands on the ball. After batting it back and forth in his front paws, he grabs it with his teeth (ball dangling from between fangs), saunters back to join us, and proudly drops his trophy.

"Cool, huh? He can do that for hours—well, maybe not *hours*, but you know what I mean."

I already feel a soft spot for Baxter, and I've only been here less than an hour.

Jen can't remember an incident ever happening while he's playing ball. "But once one's started, nothing can stop it. I can't get him to fetch the ball, or come to me, or even take a piece of salmon. And if I try to hold him or comfort him," she says with a sigh, "oh, it's just so pathetic. He just tucks his head in my arms and hides, and I don't even know what to do but hold him."

A single tear slips down her cheek and she looks at me as if to say, "Please, help us." I feel tears fill my eyes, as well.

Baxter's physical exam doesn't reveal much. In about

a one-inch stripe running from his lower back down to his tail, his long black coat is just a little thinner. I can feel the stubble of some broken hairs where he has bitten at the base of his rump. But his skin there looks completely normal: no redness, bite marks, scabs, or other signs of trauma that I can find. The whole time I'm examining him—completing a neurological exam; gently stretching, flexing, and rotating his joints; carefully listening to his chest and tummy—he stands on the sofa, softly purrs, and looks at me through squinted eyes, willing to endure it all for the attention. Certainly he shows no pain, joint problems, or neurological signs. Yet, from what I've learned from Jen, the video, and my physical exam, I can make a tentative diagnosis.

Baxter's signs are fairly classic for FHS (feline hyperesthesia syndrome)—a bit of hair loss from overgrooming; running away from his tail at times, as if a family of fleas were on board and attacking him; biting at his rump now and then in almost spastic fits; and a slow, insidious onset, starting with short bouts and progressing into full-blown spells that bewilder their families and the cats themselves. Some cats with FHS fiercely guard their tails from others; a gentle touch or reaching toward them can launch them into a frenzied attack. But, many more, like Baxter, are docile.

We really don't understand what causes FHS or why it happens. From watching cats like Baxter, I believe they're responding to real sensations. It's likely they feel pain, or maybe tingling, itching, or burning, but off and on, quite literally—which may be why they seem fine between fits.

Since these cats are feeling real sensations in their bodies, shouldn't they be seeing a neurologist instead of me? You would think so. As a matter of fact, most cats I've seen have done just that. Yet, invariably, neurologists find nothing wrong with these cats' nerves. There's no device or fancy test that can give a diagnosis of FHS, but that doesn't mean it isn't real or that their nerves are simply fine. It's just that we don't know where to look as of yet.

But, if isn't in their nerves, could it be it's in their heads—a misperception, a delusion, a figment of their imagination? That's the question everyone asks. And so they end up calling me.

Imagine, for a moment, without any warning you suddenly feel a stabbing pain piercing in your lower back, or an awful itch that you can't quite scratch, or a throbbing, tingling, stinging sensation—almost like when your foot falls asleep—for no reason at all, several times a day. After a few minutes (maybe more), it simply fades away and—sigh—you're fine . . . until you feel the next attack. You can't predict when it will happen, but you know it will, again and again. It's not hard to understand why these cats are stressed and nervous. So as I care for them, I try to ease their minds and bodies.

There is no single treatment that works for this condition. For some cats, trying to reduce their stress can help to lessen their clinical signs. With other cats, enriching their lives—offering activities to shift their focus—relieves their suffering remarkably. For yet others, nothing but medication can soothe their pain and still their distress.

Because Baxter's signs were severe, we began with medication while Jen put in place a plan for enriching his environment. Since his problem first began when he became confined inside, she decided to bring a taste of the outdoors to their cabin. Before she even started, though, Baxter's signs faded and then vanished within a week. No more biting. No running and hiding. Not even the faintest hint of twitching. And, beyond his physical comfort, he was undoubtedly calmer and much happier.

Spring arrived early that year. Before the snowdrifts had fully melted, as soon as Jen could shovel and scrape a swath of deck down to the wood, Baxter made up for his winter confinement. And, in keeping with her plans to make his life more interesting, Jen worked on a few improvements to the deck. On the far side where the pines reached to the cabin with a canopy of shade, Jen built a rather large wood-framed box, filled it with a thick bed of soil, and lined it with lush strips of sod. When Jen's sister, Julie, visited one weekend, she brought with her a full patio set, which they set up where the sun was fullest. Finally, Jen added two barrels planted with dwarf lemon trees, half a dozen hanging vines, and a small bubbling fountain, which she plugged in near the planter box. And by May, when the last bits of ice had thawed, the once barren deck had become a cat's oasis.

With Baxter resuming his life outdoors, we weaned him off the medication and, in the months that followed, he never showed another sign of the fits that had plagued him that first winter in Tahoe. Throughout the summer, Baxter and Jen savored their times on the deck together. While Jen ate, read, or just relaxed for an hour, Baxter would sometimes come and sunbathe by her side. Other times, he'd stalk squirrels and birds, from within the reeds of grass that grew tall within the planter box, or batted bubbles and splashed his paws at flies and bugs that landed in the fountain.

In September, winter hit early, and the paradise they loved so much was blanketed again in snow. Even with the planter box, fountain, and trees moved inside, Baxter's fits returned full force, and the pace at which they worsened was much quicker than the year before. Unable to bear her kitty suffering again, Jen asked if Baxter could resume the medication. And, as if to prove it really worked, within two weeks his fits were gone.

And so the story continued the same, winter and spring, year after year. With the first signs of thawing snow, Jen would wean Baxter off the medication, and he would thrive with his time outdoors until, months later, the winter returned.

I heard from Jen again this fall as we've kept in touch every few months or so, through all the years since we first met at their cabin. Baxter died this August at the ripe old age of sixteen. He gracefully passed away in his favorite place, resting in the grass on their deck stretched by her side. We were both especially grateful that their last few months together were in the summer, the time of year that Baxter, certainly, loved the best.

We cried together on the phone that day, but also laughed quite a bit, as Jen thought back to stories of Baxter's adventures and antics through the years. Eventually, we ran out of words and sat on opposite ends of the phone, lingering in the silence, not sure what was left to say about one cat who, in his lifetime, touched our hearts so deeply. In that moment, before we said good-bye, with thank-yous for everything and promises to keep in touch, I also knew our thanks were even more for Baxter.

Adaptability is a state of being that reflects how we adjust to the world as it changes. To adapt we must be flexible: capable of changing ourselves and willing to do so. But, beyond this, for us to adapt, we must also take some course of action—responding somehow differently in what we do or think or feel. As we adapt, we embody a new way of being.

In a world that is always changing, every being must adapt to some degree for their survival. Sometimes whole species adapt together. Every fall around September, as the warmth of the summer fades from the air, ruby-throated hummingbirds abandon the meadows and woods around our home and head southward to Mexico or even farther to Panama, where insects and spiders are plentiful. Weighing barely more than a dime and soaring past at nearly thirty miles an hour, they travel for up to two thousand miles, many flying nonstop across the wide-open seas of the Gulf of Mexico. In the early spring, they rechart their course, returning to court, breed, and nest in our woodlands. To them this remarkable, twice-a-year journey is simply a routine of life in step with nature.

In the course of my work, I find animals adapting more subtly in smaller groups or, often, by themselves. As zoo attendance swells during school breaks and the summer months, a family of three gibbons loiters higher in their habitat to avoid the crowds that throng below. Since the passing of her father

from a tragic illness just a month ago, the youngest gibbon
clings more closely to her mother. When crowds fade near
closing hour and the evening breeze weaves its way through
the trees, her older sister lures her from her mother's side to
swing and frolic in the branches near the ground. Each adapts
in keeping with the others' needs and wishes.

Oftentimes, my patients face greater hardships than other
animals. Some live in environments that oppressively limit
a range of their behaviors. Many cope with circumstances—
people, animals, or situations—that they simply find too
stressful. Still others struggle with their own limitations:
diseases, injuries, or behavioral conditions that cripple their
bodies and hinder their lives. For many I see, these hardships
happen in concert. What touches me in watching my patients is their willing acceptance of the challenges they meet,
regardless of how daunting they would be to me. Some people
could proclaim that these animals have no choice. Others
might say that they lack the will to resist their fate—they
simply surrender to whatever they are given. But what I see
in my patients is tolerance, acceptance, and willingness to
adapt to whatever life brings them day to day.

An old folktale from Korea speaks to me deeply about adapting. When Yuk On's husband first returned home from being
away for many years at war, she was overjoyed that, at long
last, he had returned home safe. After several weeks, however, her relief gave way to worry. Each morning as Tae Hyun

woke, Yuk On met him with an adoring smile and a tender kiss to begin their day as she had always done. Where before, in turn, he would wrap her in his arms and hold her, now he stiffened and turned away without a word. During dinner, when they used to share stories and tales about their day, he now sat in stony silence as he picked and nibbled at his food. And at nighttime, if she snuggled close, he shrugged her off and faced the ceiling or rolled away to the edge of the bed, leaving Yuk On to lie alone. In most every way that she could tell, Tae Hyun seemed a different man from the husband who had left for war.

With the passing of each week, Tae Hyun's manner appeared to worsen, and Yuk On's worry gave way to a nagging sense of doubt and fear. Her heart ached in loneliness for the husband she knew had loved her so dearly and cherished their marriage as much as she, for Yuk On was certain this ghost did neither. She grieved for her soul mate who was lost in battle, and resented this shadow who took his place.

Late one night as Tae Hyun lay sweating and murmuring in his dreams, Yuk On felt she could not bear another night feeling so alone. She dressed in an overcoat, left their home, and wandered along the streets of the village. After a while, despite the late hour, she came across a small, dimly lit house. Yuk On recognized it at once as the home of Hyeja, a village elder.

"Of course," she whispered to herself, as she dared to softly knock on the door, for Hyeja was known throughout the village for his special talent with potions and charms. Thinking she heard a faint reply, Yuk On carefully tried the latch and, when it clicked, edged the door open. In front of her, the old man sat wrapped in a blanket and huddled by a fire.

While tending the flames, the old wizard asked, "What brings you here at such an hour, my child?" Then, without turning, he waved for her to join him.

As soon as she sat with him on the floor, Yuk On burst out her entire story, along with her deepest worries and fears. Through it all, the old man listened and, every so often, silently nodded.

"Please help me bring back the dear Tae Hyun that I married," Yuk On pleaded. Then, before he could respond, she added, "There must be something you could give me to help me fill his heart again—a charm, an amulet . . . a potion?"

At last, spent from exhaustion, she sat and faced the elder in silence.

"I believe I know a potion that can bloom your husband's love again," Hyeja replied in almost a whisper. "But to make it, you must bring me the whisker of a living tiger."

Yuk On sat in stunned silence, searching his face. Surely she must have heard him wrong.

"A tiger?" she asked.

The old man nodded.

"But that would be impossible!" she blurted. "Certainly, there must be something else—"

"If it is truly your heart's desire," the wizard assured her with a smile, "you will find a way, my child."

Yuk On left Hyeja's house as lost and desperate as when she'd arrived. Wandering through the roads and alleyways of

her village, she felt defeated before she started. Yet, somewhere on her way back home, she fancied a plan that, if it
worked, would give her a tiger's whisker for the potion.

The following morning, as soon as Tae Hyun left their
home to work in the fields, Yuk On dashed to the village
market to buy several pieces of meat from the butcher. She
then rushed home to continue her day.

Late that night, once Tae Hyun had finally nodded off to
sleep, Yuk On quietly slipped out of bed, dressed, stuffed the
meat in her pack, and fled through the streets of the sleeping
village. Once she passed the last house in town, guided by
the light of the moon, she followed a rugged, well-worn path
winding upward into the mountains.

After an hour of steady hiking, the trail crossed over a
rocky ridge. Just ahead, the path dropped into a wooded valley veiled in mist. The air grew moist with the rich scent of
cedar and a layer of fir needles blanketed the ground, muffling
Yuk On's footsteps so she could barely hear them, as if the
shadows in the trees were conspiring to conceal her.

At the far side of the valley, the trail resumed its upward
climb, and Yuk On stopped to take in the scene. The trees
and fog gave way to a clearing blanketed with tall grasses and
reeds. Along the face of the sheer rock wall, a narrow ledge
ran the length of the meadow, and just above it a faint, dark
shadow perched overlooking the valley below. In that instant, Yuk On knew she'd reached her destination, for stories
of travelers through the years had told of that same shadow
just above the glen and the den of a tiger that lay deep
within it.

Half-relieved to have found her goal and half-terrified to go any farther, she edged her way around the meadow until she reached the rocky wall. Much too close for Yuk On's comfort, she could easily see the ledge above and the entrance to the cave just within the shadow. She could feel her heart racing as she left the shelter of the woods and tiptoed through the meadow to a small, barren patch. Carefully, quietly, Yuk On reached into her pack and neatly laid the meat in an offering on the ground. Then, as quickly as she dared, she traced her way back through the grass to take cover in the shadows of the trees that lined the glen.

To Yuk On is seemed that eons passed, as she stood among the brambles and branches in the wood. She began to wonder if the cave had been abandoned or, perhaps, the stories were nothing more than myths, spun long ago by adventure-seeking travelers. But then something—a dark shape—appeared within the shadow. More massive and imposing than she'd dared imagine, it paused for a moment at the edge of the cave. Then it took a step forward and its face came alive. The tiger emerged from the dimness around him, surveying the valley and ridges beyond. His eyes stared intently each place they landed. His whiskers, stiff in every direction, reflected the light of the moon. His ears seemed to point wherever he looked, poised to pick up any nuance of sound. Except for the faint sound of trickling water from a brook that ambled in between the reeds, the valley stared back at the tiger in silence.

The tiger turned his gaze to the forest near Yuk On. His eyes pierced through the darkness around her. His nose seemed to twitch, alert to her fear. And though it seemed hard to believe, Yuk On knew he somehow could smell her presence. Then, leaping from the narrow ledge, he bounded down the rocky wall—far too quickly and easily—and landed in the meadow where she'd left her gift. He turned, snuffled, and chuffed in Yaku's direction and then at the ground around where he stood. With each sniff, he seemed to consider the meat, the meadow, and Yuk On deliberately.

She barely saw him bite at the food. But, within a few gulps, he'd eaten it all. And then he was gone, blending into the reeds, just another shadow in the moonlight. A minute passed and then another—no trace of the tiger—and then he appeared, an outline on the mountainside far upon the ridge.

As soon as she no longer could see the tiger, Yuk On left her hiding place and scampered back the way she came, down the mountain and on to the village. Then, at last, she was home and under the covers without Tae Hyun even knowing she'd been gone. And, in spite of the thrill of her adventure and relief of making it safely home, she fell fast asleep as her head hit the pillow.

In the days and weeks that followed, Yuk On kept to the same routine, hiking late at night to make her offering to the tiger. One night, however, as Yuk On walked into the clearing, she found the tiger perched just above her—stretched along the narrow ledge, watching her arrive. Afraid to take another step, she stopped midstride to weigh her choices: freeze and wait for him to leave, however long that may take; flee and risk the chance that running could spur the tiger to chase her; or slowly retreat and miss a night—but then

what? All the while, the tiger stared—focused, waiting, stat-
uesque—as she stood frozen, still as a scarecrow.

In spite of how his gaze unnerved her, Yuk On knew what
she must do. Bowing her head, she continued, step by step,
to the usual spot, discreetly laid the meat on the ground, and
steadily walked back to the forest. When Yuk On turned,
she was startled to find the tiger had already left the ledge.
Quickly scanning the clearing, half-expecting him to pounce
from nowhere, she found him again, standing over her offering. He sniffed at the clearing where Yuk On had stood,
paused to consider it, and then ate the snack. While gulping
the last bite and licking at his whiskers, he turned to look her
way for a moment and then padded off in the other direction.

Each trip from that night on, the tiger already lay on the
ledge, surveying the clearing, when Yuk On arrived. Just
as before, once she left for the forest, the tiger leapt from
his resting place, ate, and shortly wandered off. And then
one night he wasn't there. Yuk On scanned the ledge, the
meadow, the mountains, the edge of the forest. No matter
where she looked, she couldn't see the tiger. So, with nothing else to do, she continued to her offering spot to leave
the meat just as before. Then, as she turned to leave, she
heard him chuff that distinctive breath she'd noticed from
across the meadow. Still bent over, she slowly turned to find
him standing right beside her, utterly blended within the
grass and reeds around him, except for a flash of his eyes and
two thin strips of orange and black running in circles around
his cheeks and upward toward his forehead. Facing the tiger

eye to eye, her heart pounding so loudly that she could hear it pulsing, Yuk On stood, breathed, and turned heroically toward the woods. As she walked back through the meadow, the tiger seemed indifferent, content to focus on his evening snack.

From that point forward, when Yuk On arrived, she found the tiger waiting at her offering spot. Within a week he even ate before she left the meadow for the woods and, when this happened, Yuk On knew it was finally time to take her chance. The following night, as she bent to leave the meat, she pulled a pair of scissors from her pocket. The tiger approached as he had each night before, and when he lowered his head to sniff her offering, she reached toward his muzzle with the scissors. The tiger simply ate, unfazed, and, to Yuk On's amazement, in her palm lay a whisker. Once he finished eating, the tiger chuffed once more, this time sniffing at Yuk On's hand, and then without a pause, padded off and upward toward the ridge.

Amazed, relieved, and happier than she'd imagined, Yuk On ran—and almost skipped—the entire way back to the village. As she reached the wizard's house, she found it dimly lit once more. She knocked and heard his voice, as she had done many nights before. Running to his side and waving the whisker, still clutched in her hand, she burst out, "Here it is! Can you believe it? I have the tiger's whisker for you!"

Kneeling beside him on the floor, Yuk On proudly laid it in his hands.

Examining the whisker thoughtfully, the old man said, "I can see, indeed, it is a tiger's whisker; but tell me, my child, how did you come by this?"

Yuk On told him of all she had done in the months since she last saw him. As before, the old man listened and, every so often, quietly nodded. Then, without a word, he tossed the whisker in the fire.

Yuk On watched, too stunned to speak, as the whisker curled and shriveled to nothing but ashes. Then she collapsed at the old man's feet and sobbed, "How could you do this after all I've done? I must have that potion. I must . . . I must . . ."

Taking her face into his hands, he wiped the tears from her cheeks and smiled.

"There's no reason to despair, dear child. You've no need for a potion now. In fact, you never needed one."

Bewildered and confused, she looked in his eyes as he continued, "You alone, with no one's help, tamed a wild tiger with nothing more than what's inside you—patience, commitment, and compassion in your heart." Still smiling, he added, "And a good bit of courage. If you can do this with a tiger, you can do the same with anyone.

"Go to your husband, child, and trust you have all you need within you."

As Yuk On made her way back through the village, she kept struggling with the old man's words. All that she had hoped for had fizzled in the flames. How could he compare a wild tiger with her distant husband? But, as Yuk On slipped between the sheets and turned to Tae Hun's side, she smiled.

It seems part of human nature that we look to others for how they can change—husbands, wives, children, friends, the person in line at the grocery store. Often, as with Yuk On, we do so with good intention. From our viewpoint, we have the answer. *If only she would learn*, we think, *or just move off her position a bit. If only he would stop to look at my perspective for just a moment. If only the old wizard would make a magic potion.* But it's not a matter of changing them. Adapting always begins with us, when we first shift in *our* perspective.

So often, as humans, we focus on change, just like Yuk On did till the end. It's easy to empathize with her. We envision how it looks and feels and we want the change to happen now. In doing so, we make it a goal—a point in time, a certain result—something we can measure, or compare, to where we are right now. The world is always changing, though. Our circumstances are never static. Like a boat crossing the ocean, we're never precisely on the right course. We drift a little off to starboard, then shift our way a bit to port— always correcting, adjusting, refining. Adapting is an ongoing process. There is no endpoint. It's always evolving.

As I watch animals, I see they get this. It's not that they don't have objectives, but they adjust them more willingly than we do. While we hold focused on our goal, animals accept adapting as a process, adjusting their plans according to each situation. Throughout the many months of Yuk On's journey into the mountains, the tiger adapted with remarkable ease. More than once, he surprised Yuk On by accepting her before she was ready. Trusting his instincts, he adapted to her presence, thoughtfully and with intention.

Baxter touched me deeply, in part because of how he adapted with poise and grace to every situation. As long as he was by Jen's side, he accepted each day for what it brought. Back in Arcadia, when Jen was at school, he adjusted quite contentedly to roaming the neighborhood and the woods. In those four years, he became quite skilled at stalking chipmunks and hapless birds. Even so, at the end of the day, when Jen returned from class or work, reliably, he'd be back at home, waiting and ready to join her. As an indoor cat in Tahoe, he adjusted with remarkable ease—that is, until his body objected. Even when he was riddled with fits of pain and twitches that relentlessly pursued him, Baxter withstood it all with a calm and loving nature. His greatest comfort in those times was being cradled in Jen's arms. Throughout his life, he willingly adapted the best he could to each new situation while remembering what mattered most.

The wounded husband, Yuk On, and the wise man are in each of us. Deep within we all have parts that are scared, wise, and desperate for love. Each of these parts stirs within us as we go about our lives with all our plans, hopes, and wishes for the future. Yet, as we put our dreams into action, the world around us is also adapting. We have a choice whether to stay on course, fixed and locked in our intention, trying to change the world and others as needed to meet our goals; or to look around, take stock, and adjust where we are headed.

Likewise, within each of us also lies the tiger—untamed; instinctive; flexible, even before we believe we are ready; capable of accepting and adjusting to whatever happens. The creatures around us can serve to remind us that we hold the wisdom already within for how we can change our lives and open ourselves to new ways of being, if only we are willing to clip a whisker from the tiger.

7
Integrity

If you see a whole thing—it seems that it's always
beautiful. Planets, lives . . . But close up a world's all
dirt and rocks. And day to day, life's a hard job, you
get tired, you lose the pattern.
—Ursula K. Le Guin

Sakari lies perfectly calm and still, gracefully poised on the
uppermost branch of a barren eucalyptus tree. I can almost
imagine she's no longer alive, one of those taxidermic leopards on display in a natural history museum, if not for an
occasional twitch of her tail, the steady rise and fall of her
chest, and a barely imperceptible flare of her nostrils with
each breath. Her chin rests upon her paws. Her eyes gaze forward in my direction, casting their hypnotic spell—drawing
me in, urging me deeper—now and then blinking, but lacking expression . . . vacant . . . empty . . . almost lifeless.

My heart leaps into my throat, and in its wake swells a
rush of tears. Before it overwhelms me, I hold off a welling
wave of sadness and draw back farther into the shadows.
Brushing a stray tear from my cheek, I lean against the rock

wall and settle deeper into the crevice. Watching. Waiting. Searching her body, her facial expressions for even a slight hint of change in her features.

Sakari first came here five years ago along with her mate and companion, Mufasa. Though they had lived together at their former zoo, their history before that was oddly vague. From what I could gather reviewing old records, as part of an active breeding program, they were brought together from different litters and introduced as young adults. Once together, they stayed a pair throughout each move from zoo to zoo.

Almost since their arrival here, life for the pair seemed beset with troubles. Both cats faced an unsettling stream of medical issues, one after another. At first their problems, though frequent, were minor (a bit of hair loss, a few lacerations, short bouts of refusing to eat); but then through the years their issues progressed till both were diagnosed with renal disease. Mufasa's kidneys failed alarmingly fast, and he passed within only a year of his diagnosis. Though Sakari's disease had progressed much more slowly, it clearly was taking a toll on her body. And aside from her keepers, since her loss of Mufasa, Sakari lived entirely in solitude.

Native to the tropical forests of Southeast Asia and southern China, clouded leopards live their lives in seclusion, rarely—if ever—seen by man. By nature they are arboreal and so well adapted for life in the trees that Malaysians call them *harimau-dahan*, the "tree branch tiger." Historically found from Nepal in the west to the coast of the South China Sea in the east, and south to the islands of Sumatra and Borneo, they've adapted well from life in the trees to a range of terrains, from grasslands to swamps. Now, however, they are regarded as "vulnerable"—an inconspicuous way of saying that they easily could become extinct. Loss of habitat from deforestation and being hunted for their bones, meat, and fur has led to few leopards still surviving in nature outside of protected wildlife preserves.

Between the mainland and the islands, two discrete species evolved, but both share in common a skull and skeleton different from those of any other living cat. Dubbed modern-day saber-tooths because of their enormous fangs, they're as skilled at hunting monkeys and deer as were their prehistoric ancestors. Yet, they're equally as talented at stalking wild pigs and birds.

Born in litters of pairs or triplets, the kittens nurse until they are roughly five months old. And by the time they turn two, they are living fully on their own. Though little is known about how they breed in the wild, when captive they form pair bonds for life, which means Sakari has been mateless for three years.

A fly hovers around her face, lands on her nose, and then buzzes away. She blinks and sighs, but still stares off into some faraway dimension.

Where is she?

I scan her enclosure for changes.

Once again, her caretakers have already left the morning's enrichment. A fresh pile of bamboo leaves lightly spotted with brownish flecks—I suspect sprinkled enticingly with clove, nutmeg, or cinnamon—once would reliably stir Sakari to rub and roll in blissful fits. Now it sits unnoticed in a corner. A large block of ice has been placed at the base of the tree. Mottled with dark patches and tinted with a blush of red—no doubt a meatsicle seductively laced with horse meat and blood—beckons Sakari to sniff, lick, and gnaw at it. Instead it melts neglected in a slowly growing puddle. Not far below her, the pelt of a muntjac deer dangles from another branch and down to the floor. Shunning these offerings, which would easily enthrall most other cats, she lies on the branch unmoving and indifferent.

Sakari's enclosure leaves little to work with: four flat concrete walls adjoined in a simple rectangle, fifteen feet deep and thirty feet across. A row of massive plate-glass windows runs the length of the viewing wall while the painted back and side walls depict a hackneyed jungle scene. At best, the illusion is vague and weak: winding tree trunks; dangling, knotted vines; a bright green canopy above fades to muddled leaves below; deep brownish moss and a few ferns shroud the jungle floor; and darkened shadows between it all—a two-dimensional picture for visitors with nothing of interest for a cat. The eucalyptus, though long dead, reaches upward from the floor with branches spanning two of the walls. Up above, a green mesh screen overlays the entire exhibit, masking several banks of lights and the ceiling just above. And below it all, smooth concrete floors slope backward toward a grated gutter, so the pen can be easily swept and hosed.

The walls and floor surrounding me differ remarkably from Sakari's habitat. The floor beneath me is uneven and gritty. The walls where I lean, though formed from concrete, look and feel as if they are chiseled from rock. The ceiling, roughly arched and domed, comes smoothly down to meet the walls. A few canned spotlights here and there replace the rows of fluorescents above. The effect is impressive. With lights cast on the blackened walls and dimmed to a faint, amber glow, it looks and feels as if I am hiding in a cave. Yet, the contrast is painfully stark to me. Between the crevice where I sit and the eucalyptus tree, utility replaces form and ambiance yields to function.

I worry about priorities. *A zoo without a steady flow of visitors cannot survive for long. Yet, focusing on patrons before the needs of animals betrays a zoo's essential purpose.*

Sakari jerks me back from my thoughts. Her eyes are now focused. Her gaze is clearly alert and direct.

Is she watching me? I hold my breath.

She lifts her head from her paws and stares. Still as stone. No twitch of the tail. No flare of her nostrils. I can't see even a hint of her breathing. Watchful. Intent. Instincts in place and fully engaged. I envision her perched in a kapok tree tracking a dusky leaf monkey as he swings lower from the canopy above.

Relieved to see her mindful, at least for the moment, I dare not move for fear that I could jinx her, once more, causing her to withdraw into some far-off state. I breathe again with absolute silence, each breath carefully shallow and slow, as if she were the hunter and I were her prey.

I sit. She stares. Each transfixed by the other. Several minutes pass. Then as instantly as I came in her sights, she shifts her gaze and licks her paws; long, steady, casual laps at one foot then the other—first front, then rear, then on to her legs . . . her thighs . . . her tail. I dare, at last, to shift a bit, just enough to follow her movements.

That tail.

The tail of a clouded leopard is unlike that of any other cat. Though their bodies are smaller and lighter than other leopards'—somewhere in size between a bobcat and a lynx—their tails rival those of most any lion or tiger in length. That massive tail is pivotal to their lives in the jungles of southern Asia. Roughly the same length as their body, it allows them to balance high up in the trees, not only for nesting, sleeping, and leaping from limb to limb in chase of monkeys or birds, but also—when used together with uniquely flexible joints in their paws—for dashing down tree trunks headfirst, like a squirrel, and dangling from branches upside down by a single paw, while stalking unsuspecting prey passing on the ground below them. Circled with black broken rings and covered with thick fur, their tails are a seductively alluring blend of function and form.

I grimace as my eyes trace her tail from base to tip. Except for several inches at each end, Sakari's tail is thoroughly bald. No scabs. No pustules. No bite marks, ulcers, or other lesions—just hairless. And though I'd never find a tail like hers among a wild cat, this pattern is quite common among captive clouded leopards. While health, nutrition, and diseases, certainly, all play a role, the greatest cause by far for finding hair loss in these cats is stress. In zoos as well as nature, clouded leopards are keenly sensitive—more so than any other felid—to social stressors, intrusive noises, environmental changes, and human presence. In the wild, they avoid such stress by retreating deeper into the jungle or climbing up into the canopy above. Indeed, their sensitivity is the reason for their reclusiveness and why they're so rarely seen in nature. In captivity, however, they have nowhere to escape. For that matter, exhibits such as this one don't even offer them a place to hide from the steady stream of human voices and prying eyes of passersby. Add to this the dull, insipid dreariness of a small, barren pen—not to mention the loss of a lifelong companion—and it is not surprising that Sakari is distressed. The sad result is that clouded leopards far too often develop odd habits to cope with stressors they face in their lives. For reasons no one understands, these cats tend to groom their tails till after countless hours and days of grooming, they lick them bald.

Dogs lick at their legs and flanks, horses crib on fences and gates, parrots pluck out their feathers, elephants weave their heads from side to side, and bears pace back and forth along the walls of their enclosures. Patterns of behavior like these are not compulsions, as we saw with Dougal, but, instead, quirky habits some animals repeat, over and over and over again. Unlike as we see with OCD, most quite willingly stop if distracted or redirected to another activity. If not, however, they repeat these behaviors, oftentimes for hours a day. Their patterns vary one way or another, and so they look less ritualized than do those of animals with compulsions. These stereotypies, as scientists call them, occur with no relation at all to what is happening in the moment. In other words, they serve no purpose. But it's not a mystery how they develop.

Conflict, frustration, crowding, stress, or simply a lack of any-thing new or interesting in their lives can put an animal at much greater risk for developing one or more of these habits.

Odd behaviors such as these are not just seen in animals. We see similar patterns in humans—at times with boredom, frustration, or stress, but sometimes for no apparent reason. Many people chew gum well beyond any "fresh breath" taste: Some chomp furiously; some blow bubbles, popping and snapping them out of habit or delight; others gnaw methodi-cally for hours, almost like a cow, gently and patiently chew-ing on her cud. On airplanes, in lecture halls, at movies, and in restaurants, I see people sitting in chairs and shaking their feet side to side or up and down, some intensely and others gracefully, back and forth, pausing, then resuming back and forth again. At one time in my younger days, I could lecture to a class only if I was pacing in front of the room, side to side or around in circles—not unlike a wolf walking a well-worn path in his enclosure. Pause too long in any one place and my train of thought just seemed to vanish. (Fortunately, some conditioning and a few speakers' courses broke this habit.)

Stereotypies also develop when animals cannot perform a natural range of behaviors for their species. Think of any ani-mal and we can sort what they do in a day into various basic behavior groups: hunting or foraging; eating; traveling; rest-ing; sleeping; maintenance activities (for example, seeking shelter, eliminating, grooming); and social behaviors (such as communicating, breeding, and playing). Research has shown that farm cats, for example, sleep and rest for more than half their day. They hunt for roughly four hours daily and spend a

bit less than another four grooming. Eating, traveling, playing, and other behaviors combined take less than two hours.
From lions to ocelots, these numbers do not vary much from
what I observe with wild cats in the zoo or, for that matter, what clients report when they track their cats' behaviors
at home.

Feed a house cat free choice from a bowl with no incen-
tive to search for food, and he will spend more time in the
day resting, grooming, or seeking attention. Keep a clouded
leopard confined to an enclosure without a choice of trees to
climb, reasons to explore where she lives, and a hiding place
or two, and she may well end up like Sakari.

We can plot out a time budget for an animal in any setting
and predict what might happen if we limit what they can do.
I look at these behavior groups as if they're each spokes on
a wheel. If one is shortened, for whatever reason, the wheel,
once round, becomes misshapen, and the animal's life spins
out of balance.

When one behavior is not expressed, another behavior
will take its place. Animals, of course, are living beings and
not unwitting automatons, performing only what they're pro-
grammed to do. To fill the void of what is missing, they'll
draw from their behavioral repertoire. A cat that can't hunt
will likely forage—but if he's given no reason to, he may well
groom more, sleep, or pace. As such, it's not at all surprising
that Sakari licks her tail for hours. What else has she to do?
What can she to look forward to? Can a keeper's daily visits
fill the gap left by Mufasa? How does she deal with a constant
stream of people staring at her from across the glass—tapping

their fingers to see her response, pointing, growling, roaring, laughing? To me it's no wonder that she retreats into some distant world, far away from prying eyes, within a jungle of her own.

In the rain forests of Thailand and Borneo there are no clouded leopards missing hair on their tails. Despite their reclusiveness, it is not that they aren't seen; it's simply that bald-tailed clouded leopards don't exist. Ethologists who live in the Congo for years never see western lowland gorillas regurgitate to eat their meal once more. On safari in Africa, we rarely spot giraffes licking at anything that isn't food. Likewise, in the Arctic Circle, polar bears don't pace on ice floes, retracing their footsteps time and again. And yet, we do see these behaviors develop from time to time in zoos.

Twenty years ago, I avoided some zoos for good reason. Times were different then and, all too often, what I saw haunted me long after my visits. At that stage in my career, freshly out of vet school, I lacked the prowess and expertise to know how I could make a difference. Yet, struggling with my ghosts at night, I also couldn't surrender to them. And so I resolved to work within zoos, using what unsettled me to inspire the changes I longed to see.

For at least five thousand years, humans have captured and collected animals from the wilderness. As far back as 3000 B.C. in Mesopotamia, the ruling class caught elephants and apes to keep for hunting on private reserves. Dignitaries from faraway lands came with gifts of exotic creatures as symbols of their dominion and wealth. Venturing into the deserts around them with packs of greyhounds and lassos in hand, the pharaohs in nearby Egypt caught lions to worship and raise as mascots. Across the globe in distant China, successions of emperors' dynasties fashioned elaborate palace gardens to harbor their royal menageries.

Across cultures and through the ages, humans have collected countless creatures from the wild for nothing more than entertainment. Once the domain of only the wealthy till as late as the eighteenth century, few in the public ever saw these collections. In fact, the oldest zoo standing today, the Tiergarten Schönbrunn in Austria, was founded from the emperor's menagerie. But, as soon as the common folk got a chance to see these animals face-to-face, public zoos quickly became a crowd-pleasing global phenomenon.

It was not until the 1970s, though, with the dawning of the Aquarian age, that zoos began to rethink their purpose. A paramount shift took off at that time and still, very much, is unfolding today. Although they will likely always be striving to entertain their visitors, today's zoos and wild animal parks focus to a large degree on conservation. With the rolls of endangered species growing from hunting, poaching, and habitat loss, a central mission of modern zoos is protecting animals in the wild from extinction. And to that aim, hand in hand with conservation, zoos now strive to educate their guests. Docents offer crocodile skulls, waterbuck horns, and teeth from wolves for visitors to touch and hold. Zookeepers schedule training sessions late in the morning when crowds are largest, to show how teaching a new behavior can make a seal's life more interesting. Overnight stays give families a chance to learn, play, and discover together; fall asleep under the stars with lions or tigers murmuring in the distance; and wake to the songs of gibbons swinging through the ropes at dawn as they explore their habitat.

Behind the scenes, the work at zoos goes far beyond what the public sees. What impresses me most wherever I travel is the zoo staff's commitment and passion for the animals. Working long hours for modest wages and, almost always, in unglamorous conditions, zookeepers, to me, are unsung heroes: raking old hay and adding new bedding; ensuring each animal is cared for and healthy; hauling; sweating; worrying; cleaning and raking again; endlessly offering new challenges and puzzles; feeding a confounding assortment of diets, each handmade expressly for the animals' needs—the lemurs savor peanut butter, mealworms, and biscuits; the binturongs eat chicken, grapes, oranges, and kiwi; and the zebras graze on grass hay, alfalfa cubes, and a bit of oats. Keepers, trainers, zoo vets, and curators all work in concert with one goal in mind: the health and well-being of the animals in their care.

Breeding programs between zoos ensure that species avoid extinction in spite of all the perils in nature and despite so many being caused by man. Without the conservation efforts of zoos toward habitats beyond their walls, many species would fatefully be one step closer toward extinction. Tragically, nonetheless, my daughter might still never get a chance to see the amazing sights I have seen in nature—a California condor soaring high above the Big Sur coast; northern sea lions south of Coos Bay, Oregon, sunning among the rocks on Simpson Reef; or green sea turtles swimming in the water and buried in the warming sands of Kahalu'u Beach.

Beyond their day-to-day operations, zoos are struggling to evolve. It's not enough for them to meet their animals' basic needs. Today's zoos must constantly question what can be done to make their lives richer. Animals in dreary, humdrum pens with walls on one side and bars on the other are relocating to inspired new exhibits planned by architects with expertise in zoo design. What once was just display is now designed as theater, as much for the animals as for their watchers. More and more, the areas for animals and visitors exist side by side and commingle as one. In a world that seems far removed from zoo paths, visitors can connect with the animals, experience the world a bit from their viewpoint, and learn about their conservation. But even more importantly, the exhibits enrich the animals' lives—changing week to week, day to day, and sometimes even more often, encouraging them to explore their world, connect with others, think, play, and adapt—in other words, find fulfillment. When I asked twenty years ago, "Do you feel the polar bears are happy?" I was met with funny looks and silence. Nowadays, I get a detailed description of all that is right and wrong in their lives.

Yet even now, far too often, I still find animals who haunt me—weaving, pacing, plucking, and licking despite the very best of intentions of the team that cares for them. When all is said and done, we expect animals to accept the limits we place on their lives. Most adjust well, but many cannot.

They are not living in the wild. Perhaps if they were, they wouldn't survive with mounting threats of global warming, habitat loss, and man's exploitation. Even so, as their captors and keepers, it's up to us to make things right. We must ensure their needs are met and their lives are fulfilled in every dimension.

Our responsibility to animals is really no different in our own homes. Though dogs and cats are domesticated, their needs and behaviors echo those of their wild cousins. So, I draw the same spokes and wheel for house cats as for clouded leopards. Yet, even more often in our homes than at zoos, I find animals whose lives are out of balance. From wild creatures to family pets, the symptoms are very much alike.

I think of Pandora and Persephone, found as kittens less than six weeks old. Amy, a veterinary technician, had brought them into the clinic where she worked after finding them stranded in a vacant lot. Pausing at the street corner for traffic during her morning run, she heard their tiny voices calling from somewhere off between the bushes. When she left the curb to track the sound, she found the kittens in a cardboard box, desperately clawing at the sides to escape. A small plastic cereal bowl lay toppled beneath their feet, empty except for a few thin, crusty smears of something on the underside. Amy hoped they were smudges of food. A bottle of water lay on its side, its lid popped open, half-empty and wrapped within a damp, mildewed kitchen towel; as she crouched down to the box, she could smell its sour, acrid odor.

The kittens' clawing became more desperate and their mews turned into plaintive yowls. Amy looked up and scanned the lot—no trace of their mother, though she couldn't be sure the queen was not off in search of some type of food for the kittens. Kneeling beside the box and lifting the smallest of the pair—a girl—she instantly knew the kitten hadn't eaten for days. As she felt her tiny ribs beneath the shabby, matted fur, Amy wondered just how long a kitten her age could live without food . . . and what had happened to her mother. She gathered some skin on the back of the kitten's neck and pulled it gently, as she had done countless times with other animals at work, and even before letting it go, she knew the kitten was badly dehydrated. Setting the girl cat down in her lap, she reached down into the box for the other, who had somehow managed to scramble halfway up and almost out, and lifted her—another girl.

Looking around the lot again, she still saw no sign of their mother. In all good conscience, she knew she couldn't take the chance of leaving until she could return to check on them sometime later that afternoon. With surgeries booked before appointments, she also couldn't be late for work. So, fate, it seemed, had taken a hand and dumped the kittens into her lap. While Amy held the second girl, the first one clambered back into her arms. As she cursed herself for deciding to jog a different route that particular morning, the kittens squinted up at her with pathetic looks of pleasure that could not have been more heartrending if they had been rehearsed. And so in spite of her resistance, Amy swaddled them in the sleeves of her sweatshirt and dashed home to get ready for work.

At the clinic, Dr. Dougherty quickly confirmed Amy's suspicions. The kittens mustn't have eaten for days and, tenting their skin as Amy had earlier, agreed that both were dehy-drated. Based on their condition, he reassured Amy that the kittens, in all likelihood, had been abandoned without their mother. The wet towel, smears of cat food, and half-empty water bottle all pointed to someone leaving the kittens with a misguided hope that some kindhearted passerby would res-cue them. Of course, the logic of placing the kittens between the bushes in a vacant lot was lost on both Amy and Dr. D., in spite of the fact that the strategy had worked.

With several helpings of baby food, a fair amount of subcu-taneous fluids (for which the kittens squirmed impossibly), and a good bath—since both were riddled with fleas that skittered amid the shampoo bubbles before being rinsed, half-drowned, down the drain—the kittens blissfully snuggled together, swaddled in a blanket in the back of a cage. Bellies bulging with their first meal in days and exhausted from the morning's adventures, both fell asleep to the trill of their own purring.

The two were an instant hit among the hospital staff—doctors, receptionists, and especially technicians. In only a week they gained half a pound, and by the end of two were as healthy and well fed as any kitten at eight weeks old. No longer tiny, wiry figures with massively pathetic eyes, in those two weeks they grew into their fur, with rounded tum-mies, gangly legs—quite capable of jumping and climbing all around the clinic—sharpened teeth, and ringing voices that they used without hesitation to demand freedom from their cage, food, and, most of all, attention.

Even before Dr. D. announced that they were ready for adoption, Amy found a home for both of the kittens with her parents. Within only a day of finding the pair, she'd figured out her strategy to work on her mom's and dad's sympathies. Persistently, but carefully, each time she saw her folks she gave them updates enhanced with pictures from her phone. But the deal was sealed one day at lunch, when she convinced her mother to meet her at the clinic, "and, oh, while you're here, let me show you those kittens I found." Fittingly dubbed Pandora and Persephone the day they left by all the staff without dissent, the girls Amy let out of the box took off with her parents to begin a new life.

The sisters took to their home instantly, exploring every cabinet and closet, managing even to open a few with a bit of willpower and perseverance. On the day that they arrived, Nate assigned them to Amy's old bedroom; however, the kittens had other plans, and within a week they'd joined Nate and Sheila among the blankets of their roomier bed. Her parents didn't mind, however, and were actually quite grateful for Amy's insistence that the girls would "brighten up" their otherwise boring lives.

I came on the scene almost a full year later from when the girls first moved in. But again, as with their adoption, it was only after Amy's gentle encouragement for weeks. "Maybe we should just try asking Dr. Virga if he could help."

So, I sit at their table with her records before me, enjoying the view from the eat-in kitchen to the courtyard and small garden beyond. While I listen to the Wolfersons' stories, the kittens play around our feet. Pandora has already discovered my doctor's bag, climbed in it without hesitation, found the compartment with my hidden stash of treats, and is grabbing and gnawing at the bag of freeze-dried chicken. Persephone, I have no doubt, would have joined her sister if there was room, but instead is pouncing in mock attacks at Pandora's tail whenever it swishes outside the bag.

As Nate interjects for the second time with "You know, they really aren't that much trouble," Sheila explains why she had called.

"We love them dearly, but I haven't had a good night's sleep for ages. And it's getting worse—not better."

The story, it seems, was that both sisters would reliably wake the couple sometime around four a.m. every morning. Nate would roll over and fall back asleep with his head buried underneath one of the pillows. Sheila, a lighter sleeper, was left to face the kittens.

"First I hear them crying—it's almost a sort of moaning . . . and after a while it becomes a bit grating. They just keep going on and on. . . ."

"For how long?"

She pauses. "Well, if I just lie there and cover my ears . . . maybe ten, fifteen minutes. I know—maybe that doesn't sound so long, but it gets to me after a while. I still hear them through the pillows."

"Oh, no—please—I totally get it."

"But honestly, I really do try to just ignore them. . . ."

"Okay, just so I really get picture, would you say it's kind of a yowl like this?" I launch into my best imitation of what I'd describe as a Siamese *maowll*. "Or more of a wail, maybe?" I follow up with a mournful but more insistent *weayeow*.

"Yeah, there you go—that's pretty much like it. Of course,

it's not just that. Then they start acting really hyper, running across the bed, knocking things off the bedside tables, or they go off to the bathroom counter and knock things over or onto the floor."

"Only if you ignore the crying, or do they do that no matter what?"

"Oh, no, they'll always do it . . . just sometimes they start right away and other times they'll wait for a while."

"Five, ten minutes—or more?"

"Sometimes five, maybe less. Other times, easily ten."

"Oh—so sometimes they meow for a bit, just start running around, and then go back to meowing?"

"Exactly."

"And you're still lying there with your head in the pillows?"

"It's really hard, but, yeah—unless they knock something over or pounce on my tummy."

"And then you . . . ?"

"Well, of course, I have to go and check what they got into. If they're in the bathroom, Persephone demands a drink from the faucet."

"How?"

"She meows and paws and won't leave me alone while I'm picking up whatever it is. And by then it's just like, 'Give me a break for a minute, girls!'"

"And if they jump on you, you know, back in bed?"

"Oh, they do that all the time. It's kind of like: yowl; come up to my pillow; sniff my face and rub against me; pounce around on the bed and me—sometimes around the room. Then it's often quiet for a while—that's when I get really nervous."

"Why?"

"Let's see . . . sometimes they'll knock things off the bookshelf. Oh, or our nightstands! It's like they're doing it on purpose, you know, just to see if they can get me up. I gave up keeping vases or flowers in the bedroom. Or figurines. Or things like that—anything breakable. Of course, sometimes they go off to the living room and then, sure enough, I'll hear something fall out there."

"When do they finally give up?"

"Oh, they don't. I mean, they'll stop for a while if I give in and feed them, but then they start up again, maybe an hour later—just as I'm falling asleep again—maybe not even that long. And it's so unfair. Nate sleeps through it all."

A picture is jelling in my mind. I turn to Nate. He raises his eyebrows, sheepishly smiles, and takes a sip of coffee. Around the edge of his cup, I watch his cheeks begin to blush. Then, I turn back to Sheila.

"And if you lock them out of the bedroom?"

"Oh, all night long, howling off and on, first that one"— she points to Persephone—"then the other, or both. And then, of course, knocking things over in the living room—off the piano or the bookshelves or the tables—or in the den."

"Amy's room, the kitchen?"

"Oh, gosh! Thank goodness not the kitchen—at least not very often—or Amy's room . . . or, really, anywhere else. It's like they hover around the bedroom door."

"I think you've got it, right there."

At some level, she already knew the answer. What Pandora and Persephone are doing is really fairly common: a classic mixture of play behaviors with attention seeking intended for their humans. She and Nate had already wondered if it might be one or the other. So, before calling me they had tried the typical tactics: locking the sisters out of the room—they cried and pawed at the bedroom door off and on, all night long; cuddling with them to calm them down—they didn't want to snuggle at playtime; feeding them extra food at bedtime—no difference; spritzing them with a squirt gun—they just ran off and played in the bathroom; and, of course, ignoring them, which certainly was the best idea, but, just like with many other clients, they didn't do this long enough or with any consistency. So, by giving in sooner or later, Sheila was, in effect, teaching the kittens, "Just try long enough. Don't give up. And if you keep at it, I'll give you attention." And, like good kittens, the girls learned their lesson well.

The solution for the sisters' behavior is really quite simple for the humans and cats: Give the kittens challenges and reasons to explore their home every day and even more each evening. Offer the girls all sorts of adventures so they won't turn to Nate and Sheila for attention. The kittens' first task will be to find their meals—no more big bowls of kibble, most of all not at four a.m.; instead, the girls will need to search their home for several smaller portions, which added together will make up their meals.

"Two important caveats," I stress as we discuss the details. "If anything, make it easy at first—put the food in rooms other than the kitchen, but still not hard at all to find. Once they catch on, you can make it more difficult, but just bit by bit. Build up to hiding the bowls and truly making it a challenge. After all, if they were kittens living on a farm, no mouse or lizard would walk up, lie down, and say, 'Okay. It's time to eat me.' They'd have to forage or hunt for their food."

As I watch Nate's and Sheila's faces, they look at me as if to say, "That's it?"

Refocusing my thoughts, I press on, "The second condition: Don't keep using the same hiding spots every day. Keep mixing things up. Find new places and switch them for the old ones—behind that cabinet; over there on that bookshelf; in this corner, here between the window and the pantry."

I then outline an enrichment program to put in place, with a good range of puzzles and challenges to keep the girls busy, especially before bedtime. Finally, I suggest closing the kittens in Amy's bedroom overnight, with water, a litter box, and a puzzle or two, to help the kittens shift their routines. The rest is up to Nate and Sheila. Only time and their diligence will tell. Although I trust they will keep me posted, I ask them to call every few weeks to keep me up to date.

Sheila calls me ten days later. As soon as phones begin ringing that morning, my assistant, Donna, comes into the treatment room. "It's Sheila Wolferson on line one. I think you better take her call."

An alarm goes off in my gut—*so soon?*

"Dr. Virga? It's Sheila Wolferson."

"Hi there." I remind myself to breathe. "What's going on?"

She hesitates. I hear her take a sip of something, and then she says, "I just can't believe the difference. I never realized how unhappy they were. It's like they're entirely different cats. Really."

She goes on to describe the changes she's seen in little more than a week. After a couple of nights of a few complaints and crashing books, the kittens now sleep quietly all night long in Amy's room. When Sheila opens the door in the morning, she finds them comfortably snuggled in Amy's bed. The games, puzzles, and hunts for food keep them busy for hours each day, so by the evening all they care to do is cuddle. At bedtime, with Pandora in Nate's arms and Persephone in Sheila's, the Wolfersons carry the sleepy-eyed cats to Amy's room and tuck them in.

"It's a complete transformation," she adds.

In the months and years that follow, the girls still thrive with those simple changes we made in their lives. Though Pandora and Persephone have long since fully grown and are free to sleep where they wish, many times they still prefer to camp in Amy's bed. Now, no matter which room the cats choose, though, all in the family sleep through the night.

The Wolfersons' cats adjusted well to their home. Sakari did not to her habitat. Of course, their situations and circumstances were very different—for that matter, so were their genetics. Clouded leopards and house cats sit at opposite ends of a spectrum of felids. Given their species, when their needs weren't met, each tugged further toward their end of that spectrum. The kittens, already social creatures, demanded even more attention. Sakari, reclusive as a cat can be, withdrew even further from everything around her.

Perhaps their greatest difference, though, lay in how their lives were managed. Regardless of all her keepers' efforts, the limits set by Sakari's enclosure were just too oppressive for her to overcome. It failed to meet her most basic needs. The kittens' home, in contrast, was rich with opportunities. All it took was to give their human family guidance.

Integrity is a state of being whole and undiminished. Living with integrity requires that we are honest with ourselves and others about our needs and wishes. Yet, it also means that we fulfill those truths by living them. When we deprive ourselves of our basic needs, we stop living in integrity and our lives become diminished.

Animals by their very nature do not restrict their lives by choice. Yet humans do—in countless ways—with animals, others, as well as ourselves. We have few, if any, captors or keepers, although we act as if we do. Every day we put ourselves in boxes, denying ourselves the things that matter most to us.

We can look at human wants and needs as we do those of animals, plotting them on a wheel—each spoke representing a need for which we seek fulfillment: health and well-being; work or career; creativity and personal expression; relationships and connection with others; and spirituality or a sense of belonging to something greater than ourselves. Several times a year, I sketch this wheel for my own life. Each time I do, I find a spoke that is shorter than the others—something I aspire to or value that is missing. Laying out the wheel helps me reflect on my own life: where it is out of balance and what

I can do to make it whole. Oftentimes, it is obvious from how I set my priorities and the choices I make from day to day. I skip running to give myself a bit more time to write, setting my creative time ahead of my physical well-being. I leave earlier for the zoo in place of breakfast with my family, trading connection and relationships for work. I miss my morning meditation time to sleep a little later, and all day long I feel less grounded in how I relate to others. Each of these choices may by themselves seem trivial. Yet, added together, again and again, they take a very real toll on our lives. Just as with the animals I see, when we live with integrity, we improve our lives in every dimension: body, mind, and spirit.

As we strive toward integrity, we run into conflicting needs. Yet, staying true to our highest values helps us to reconcile them. As M. Scott Peck wrote in *The Different Drum*:

> *Integrity is never painless. It requires that we let matters rub against each other, that we fully experience the tension of conflicting needs, demands, and interests, that we even be emotionally torn apart by them.*

And farther in the book, Dr. Peck continues:

> *As soon as we think with integrity we will realize that we are all properly stewards and that we cannot with integrity deny our responsibility for stewardship of every part of the whole.*

We can find wholeness and balance in our lives only when we attend to all our needs and our highest values. We must be stewards to ourselves, honoring what most fulfills us.

We can turn to the animals in our lives who live within boundaries that we have set as humans—our pets at home; horses in the stable; creatures at the zoo; a flock of sheep grazing in a meadow—to consider how we have limited their lives, defining what they can and cannot do at any moment. The ways by which we put constraints on their existence reflect how we set limits on our own. And how we bring them greater fulfillment is really no different from how we do so with ourselves—through careful attention to every part of the whole.

If we're willing to consider the animals around us and take notice of where we limit their lives, we can better see how we set limits on ourselves. And where we bring them opportunities to find fulfillment in their lives, we can be inspired to create our own new ways of being. When we take the time to step back a moment and look at our priorities—those parts of our lives and daily routines that mean the very most to us—we can see where our lives are out of balance and adjust them to living with integrity. We begin by noticing and caring for every part of the whole.

8
Forgiveness

Cᴜⅉⅉⅉⅉⅇ

Forgiveness is not an occasional act;
it is a permanent attitude.
—Martin Luther King, Jr.

Bengals are unique among cats, a result of crossing a few domestic breeds with the leopard cat, a small, wild species native to the mainland and islands of Southeast Asia. As with any breed or species, the behavior of a Bengal cat is inextricably linked to this heritage. Even with humans, simply put, our genetics predisposes the way we think and act. How a cat interprets and relates to their world is directly impacted by their ancestry. A cat's breed traits and background, though seemingly obscure and oftentimes dismissed as distant history, can be crucial details as I work with a patient.

From the cooler taiga woodlands of Manchuria to the misty, ancient rain forests of Palawan, leopard cats live solitary, reclusive lives deep among the trees. Even when they craft their dens under roots and in small caves near villages, their size and nighttime habits conceal them well from the eyes of most humans. Yet, in those rare instances when a passerby sees one chasing a mouse through the thick of the undergrowth or stalking a lizard climbing up a tree trunk, their spotted fur can leave quite an impression. In fact, the beauty of their coats is what brought humans to capture some with hopes of conceiving the Bengal breed and bestowing this look on domestic cats.

After four generations of crossbreeding, diluting the genes of the wild cat, the marriage was deemed successful. Although they retain the spotted leopard coat of their wild ancestors, Bengals are social and affectionate. Yet, as I work with them, I sense a shadow of the wild cat lurking within their intelligence, energy, and inquisitiveness.

By appearance alone, Maurice and Jacques were unmistakably Bengals, each bearing strikingly brilliant spotted coats. But even though they looked very much alike in pattern—almost as if bookends—I very quickly recognized their differing personalities. Both cats, not surprisingly, were curious about their visitor as I leaned back in the sofa and opened up their files, but Jacques was decidedly more confident, rubbing against my leg and nudging his face into my bag. Meanwhile, his brother peered remotely from the doorway leading from the hallway to the living room. Both calm and curious, Maurice appeared content to watch us from the distant comfort of his post.

Joan and Ian Lawson first adopted the kittens directly from their breeder at about nine weeks of age. As littermates and young adults, the brothers had always been affectionate and close. Wherever one cat ventured, his brother soon would follow. At mealtimes, snack times, and playtimes with

toys—even in the midst of frantic chases round the house—
they willingly shared everything with good-natured affection. Even when napping, they lay rump to rump, their tails
intertwined most places they slept. Hisses and growls, heard
at times even between the best of friends, were utterly absent
between Maurice and Jacques. Clearly, their breeding had
eclipsed their wildcat lineage.

True to their Bengal pedigree, the cats were equally affectionate with their owners. Breakfasts were a family affair,
with the brothers often lingering underneath the kitchen table for tidbits of bacon or morsels of sausage. Most evenings
during reading time, Maurice curled up in Ian's lap while
Jacques stretched out in Joan's, or if not, they'd be close by,
draped on the arms and cushions of the sofa. Apart from safaris in the hush of night, the brothers, Joan, and Ian shared
the Lawsons' king-size bed; ensconced on the pillows or beneath the covers—particularly on cold winter nights—both
cats seemed happiest when the other was nearby.

Equally mischievous since kittenhood, they claimed the
tops of cabinets as perches, wallowed in puddles left in sinks
and bowls, and ransacked tidy stacks of laundry into muddled
jumbles of clothes. Nooks behind the living room curtains
were launching points for mock attacks, and closet doors left
ajar became gateways to secret lairs. No corner of the Lawsons' apartment remained uncharted in their exploits.

Over the years, a close-knit accord, punctuated by the
brothers' antics, became the norm for the Lawson family. But one November evening after seven years of peace,

Joan and Ian returned home to find a very different arrangement. The cats, usually at the door to greet them with trills, nudges, and rubs, were conspicuously absent and the air in the apartment seemed oddly hushed. In place of the cats, a large, ceramic urn, which normally stood in a corner of the entry, lay shattered on the floor. Though the couple was surprised by the wreckage, this was certainly not the first time they'd come home to mishaps from the cats' escapades. Half-bewildered, half-amused, they called out their names, inviting the cats to come and join them. Their calls were met with utter silence.

While Ian gathered the shards of clay, Joan decided to scout the apartment and find out what the brothers were up to. Living room, bedrooms, study, den—she found no further casualties or any other evidence of misadventures, but also no sign of the cats. Extending her search to the bathrooms and closets, Joan expected she might be prey to their pouncing from a hiding place, as had happened countless times before. Yet, curiously, she called from room to room with no response.

Converging in the kitchen with Ian (him holding a garbage bag full of dust and fragments), they found Jacques perching on a bar stool. But, as he turned to greet them, both Joan and Ian stopped cold in their tracks. Instinctively, they felt as if some other creature had entered the room. Standing poised, as if ready to pounce, Jacques glared at them unsettlingly. His pupils were wide. The glow of his retinas from the dim kitchen light shone an eerie iridescent green. There was something about the shape of his face, the set of his jaw that seemed broader and wider.

"It was almost as if," Joan recalled, "we were looking at a wildcat."

But then as soon as they called his name, his expression transformed to that of their Jacques, the cat they had known since he was a kitten. His eyes grew browner, his face quickly softened, and he trilled his familiar greeting while jumping from the stool to meet them. Leaping into Ian's lap as they crouched to pet him, he melted, softly purring, when they rubbed his chin and neck. While coddling him affectionately, Ian quizzed Jacques on what had happened and the whereabouts of his brother. He responded lackadaisically by kneading his paws on Ian's arm.

As Joan rose to continue her search, Jacques briefly glanced up to her and then toward a far corner of the kitchen. Tracing his gaze, she spotted Maurice—two eyes dimly peering down at them from above the uppermost cabinet. In a gap no larger than a small hat box, he watched them furtively but steadily. Cooing his name as if soothing a child, Joan was puzzled by his response. He remained in his roost—quiet and pensive. Ian, joining in, met with no more success. Their appeals to coax him down were useless. All the while, in the midst of their pleas, Jacques rested comfortably in Ian's arms, blithely purring contentedly.

Maurice acquiesced and joined the family only after Ian scaled the cabinets to rescue him. Standing tiptoe on the countertop to peek above the molding, Ian found Maurice tucked improbably into the corner as tight as he could fit.

But acting as if it were merely routine, he freely leapt into Ian's arms.

Once Maurice was on the ground, Jacques quickly came over to join his brother, nudging in for his share of attention. And as the two sat side by side, Jacques idly groomed Maurice. Still in no way certain about what had occurred, Ian and Joan lifted both cats into their arms and carried them off for their bedtime routine. And as the four of them snuggled together in the covers, the oddness of the evening seemed to fade and drift away.

The following morning when they awoke began no different from any other. The brothers emerged from beneath the covers to their regular dawn patrol, inspecting each room for anything new that may have appeared during the night. They continued with their daily routine as close as always—or so it seemed—unperturbed by the events of the evening before. Yet, what the Lawsons thought was just a quirky wrinkle on one strange night proved to be much more in the coming weeks and months. At first the brothers appeared to be as inseparable as always. But, at the end of the day, more and more, whenever the Lawsons returned back home, Jacques would greet them at the door without Maurice joining him. Then, combing through the apartment, they would find Maurice in the oddest places—in the linen closet beneath the towels, behind the pillows in the guest bed, or buried under a veil of shirts and dresses in the hamper. And as Maurice began to hide at other times of day and night, Ian and Joan felt certain something must be wrong with him.

A visit to their family vet did nothing to ease their

growing concerns. No medical reason could be found to explain his peculiar behavior. For all intents and purposes, despite his whimsical seclusion, Maurice appeared to be a healthy, well-adjusted cat.

Jacques's response to this tide of events further baffled the Lawsons. At first he appeared indifferent to Maurice's eccentricities. Yet, from time to time, he would stare at his brother menacingly and growl at him, or even chase him from the room, for no apparent reason. Whether these fits of malevolence were the cause of Maurice's elusive behavior or, perhaps, in response to it, the effect was the same either way. Maurice retreated further from Jacques as well as from Ian and Joan, spending most of his day furtively shadowing the family in their routines. And in the end, with Ian and Joan both distressed by the loss of their cat and exceedingly worried about his behavior, they called me in desperation.

While I listened to the Lawsons, I shifted my focus from cat to cat, studying every dimension of their behaviors I could see. Besides the obvious—where they sat and their differences in temperament—I also was searching for any signals between Maurice and Jacques.

Despite their owners' bewilderment, each cat clearly revealed his intent. Hunched by my side in pseudo-slumber, Jacques, for his part, watched Maurice with meticulous attention. Head lowered, neck set, ears perked outward, gaze fixed on his brother—every strand of his being belied the Lawsons' impression that he was just resting. Instead, I saw an assertive cat, threatening an overt attack should his brother make the slightest misstep or dare to come in the living room.

Of course, none of this was lost on Maurice. Huddled at a comfortable distance with his legs and tail tucked well beneath him, eyes averted, and ears turned back, his body reflected a perfect blend of avoidance and fear. While not making any eye contact with Jacques, he carefully watched for the slightest change in his intention—a shift in Jacques's focus from me to him, his body tensing, a movement, a stare. His curiosity about my bag and his desire join us all were tempered by prudence in the face of his brother's threat. And in my mind, Maurice transformed from a mysterious recluse to a sensible fellow. Facing the same imminent risk, I, too, would keep my distance.

I learned long ago to be very careful interpreting the relationships between two cats. Mistaking one cat as an innocent victim without recognizing his role in provoking conflict, aggression, or stress has led me along a tortuous path with frustrating and sometimes disastrous results.

To rule out Maurice's complicity, I asked the Lawsons to videotape Maurice and Jacques at random times throughout the day during the coming week—in the morning at breakfast, at the end of the day when Ian and Joan returned from work, reading time, bedtime, Sunday morning while reading the *New York Times*—as well as at various times of conflict and even when they were affectionate. Once I explained the essentials of feline facial expressions and postures, the Lawsons took on their assignment with newfound fascination for their cats.

Three weeks later, when I returned, what I watched on the video plainly confirmed what I'd seen that first day I had visited them. Day after day, the tape revealed Jacques's relentless pursuit of Maurice. At times with inconspicuous threats and at other times unabashed attacks, he doggedly harassed his brother. Quietly stretched out along Joan's side during the evening reading time, Jacques savagely pounced as Maurice jumped up near Ian's lap. Beneath the table at breakfast time while patiently waiting for pieces of sausage, he darkly scowled as Maurice watched from a respectable distance near the kitchen door. While sunning one day on the windowsill, Jacques abruptly awoke and chased Maurice with furious intensity out of the den, down the hall, and somewhere out of sight. While I could see no apparent reason—no covert signal from Maurice, no response from Ian or Joan, no extraneous sound or movement—to explain Jacques's recurrent hostility, I knew one must exist. And then, in stark contrast, at most other times he was calm, good-natured, and affectionate toward his brother.

Maurice's reaction to Jacques's fickle whims was nothing less than astounding to me. When confronted with openly fierce attacks, he would sensibly flee to take cover. Yet, in the face of less provocative threats, Maurice would cautiously stay nearby—many times even within striking range—mindfully watching for any slight shift in the ebb and flow of Jacques's temperament. Most interesting, though, when Jacques was calm, without hesitation, time after time, Maurice dauntlessly stayed by his side.

As the Lawsons watched beside me and I explained what I was seeing, I felt especially grateful to Maurice—for his forbearance and forgiveness. Time after time, in every way, he responded appropriately—many times even quite generously—allowing us to focus our attention on his brother. The diagnosis for Jacques was clear: intercat aggression. Yet, in view of how much and how often it varied, our treatment options were few.

Because environmental enrichment can handily divert an aggressor's attention, I outlined a program of constantly changing toys, treats, nests, and places to explore. Each day, we ensured Maurice had some time alone, when he could rest peacefully and safely away from the threats of his brother. When they were reunited again, as well as at family times together, the Lawsons deflected Jacques's arousal with various games and puzzles. And recognizing that Jacques's aggression was likely rooted in anxiety, I also prescribed an anxiolytic to ease his stress and constant concerns.

In those first weeks after my visits, the Lawsons' reports did not look good. Even though Maurice endured in his efforts to stay close at hand, Jacques became, if anything, more belligerent toward his brother. Although, at first, they were optimistic, Joan and Ian became more discouraged with each week that passed. So, drawing from Maurice's example of patience, forgiveness, and constancy, I urged them to stay the course.

The weeks that followed rewarded their persistence. With amazement, they watched as Jacques seemed to transform back into the cat they had once known—as giving to Maurice as his brother was to him. Always receptive to his brother's disposition, Maurice graciously responded in kind—cautiously, watchfully, and with time fully trusting. Within

months, Joan and Ian reported with glee, the brothers were
like bookends, one devoted to the other.

A dear friend of mine, Kris King, in her book *My Heart
Has Wings*, writes:

> *At its essence, forgiveness means to give as before,*
> *before the breach you experienced with another,*
> *with yourself, to once again be connected with love,*
> *respect, and appreciation. The how of it—the hard*
> *part—is owning your own part and then giving up*
> *all claims against the other, a pardon, absolution, a*
> *letting go of all blame and resentments. Forgiveness*
> *takes away the barriers that you have built and main-*
> *tained against yourself or between you and the other.*

Since I first heard Kris speak of this more than twenty
years ago, I have tried to live by this belief. In my human
frailty, though, facing the errors and slights of others as well
as my own, I find it easier to accept than put into action.

All too often, words and deeds come back to play in my
mind, long after I have offered forgiveness. Reliving that moment when I felt hurt, I let it cloud how I look at that person
as well as myself. Despite my very best intentions, often with
those I love the most, recalling the pain, I let that moment
reshape our relationship.

I am least forgiving of my own missteps. In my interactions with family and friends, strangers I meet in the course of
a day, as well as the animals in my care, I hold myself to a far
higher standard than I would expect of someone else. While

I allow myself mistakes and freely offer sincere apologies, late at night while I'm lying in bed, I linger over how I could have spoken or acted differently. In each instance, I carry those moments with me long after they have passed.

An ancient Zen parable tells of two monks who were traveling between villages. Coming to the ford of a river they needed to cross to stay on their path, they could see that the current was rapid and strong, having swelled from the melting snows of the mountaintops in spring. At the edge of the riverbank stood a young woman who'd been struggling for some time with how best to cross. Without hesitation, the elder monk approached the woman, offered to help, scooped her into his arms, and carried her across the rushing stream. After placing her safely on the far bank, she gratefully thanked him for all his help, bid him good-bye, and went on her way.

Once his fellow monk joined him after wading across the river, they continued on their journey in respectful silence. As they walked for the next few miles, the younger monk looked distracted and pensive. Finally breaking the silence, he turned at last to his elder and asked, "Brother, you know well that our vows prohibit us from any contact with women. Yet, willfully, you carried that young woman in your arms. How can this be?"

Still looking toward the path ahead, the elder was silent, but then replied, "Brother, I set her down on the bank of the river long ago. Why do you still carry her?"

As part of our human condition, each of us, in our own way, carries moments when we were hurt long after the occasion has passed. The teenager, recklessly swerving in and out of traffic, very nearly clips our fender, leaving us shaken and indignant for the rest of our commute. Remembering the birthday party we weren't invited to when we were twelve rekindles feelings of rejection years later. The words we said in anger to a loved one, in the heat of a fight, sadden us well after we've professed regret.

Engaging our complex human brain, we rethink and brood over our wounds—the words of others, what they did, and how we responded in turn. To protect ourselves from further pain, we empower these fateful moments by vowing to learn from their lessons. We infuse the memories of our hurts into our relationships, not only with our supposed offenders, but also with others in our lives.

The tolls we pay for holding on to those moments are inescapable. Resentment, anger, anxiety, and depression plague our hearts and minds. Holding those hurts in our thoughts, over time, wreaks havoc in our bodies by raising our blood pressure and heart rate, heightening pain, hampering sleep, and weakening our immune systems. The echoes of our hurt haunt us—resounding within our bodies and minds—to be relived again and again, until we choose to let them go.

Though we most often think of forgiveness as being a pardon for another, it is at least as much for ourselves—our sense of relationship, our well-being, and our peace of mind. Forgiveness, however, goes beyond letting go of blame and resentment in the moment or afterward. Forgiveness is a way of being, overlooking insults and misfortunes for our higher values: our health, happiness, and connection to others.

While animals, undoubtedly, harbor memories of pleasure, suffering, and remorse, they move past them with greater poise than humans often do. It's not that they are indifferent to insult or injury, but they more willingly return to their relationships and their lives, giving as before. For them, the continuity of their lives takes precedence. Overlooking conflict, abuse, punishment, and suffering, they offer forbearance, patience, and a readiness to forgive. Looking past missteps and blunders, they remain devoted to the enduring qualities of each relationship—companionship, sharing, and affection.

I have learned the attitude of forgiveness from many animals through the years. My own dog Katie still remains one of my greatest teachers and I am often reminded of her devotion to our relationship. Through all of our trials, even in the face of my discouragement and frustration, she remained steady and patient, forever ready to rejoin me in friendship.

When Tiffany and I first married, as is the case with many newlywed couples, our pets were our only children. At that time, our family amounted to LC, Jasmine, and Simon—three middle-aged cats, each rescued as kittens from their own heartrending histories—and Katie, a still puppylike black Labrador retriever. Katie had come into Tiffany's hands two years earlier during her internship, when a grizzled southern farmer had brought in his six-month-old puppy, then "Lucy," to be checked after being hit by a car. The bones across her right front leg, being cleanly broken and snapped in two, could be neatly repaired with surgery; but the cost of doing so was far beyond the means of the quiet old gentleman. Casting or even splinting the leg were, sadly, no more affordable for him than surgery would be. Kindly thanking the doctor for her time, his voice catching with regret, he gathered Lucy in his arms to leave with her leg unmended. Desperate to save the wounded puppy from a hopelessly misshapen leg or worse, Tiffany offered to adopt young Lucy.

Two years later, leg fully healed, Katie was the quintessential Lab, filled with boundless enthusiasm, energy, and affection. But she also suffered from profound separation anxiety, which arose from nowhere (from what we knew) within months of her third birthday. Though nothing dramatic—or minor—had changed in our lives anytime near when it surfaced, her anxiety surged fast and furious shortly after it started.

The earliest hints that something was wrong, perhaps, were subtle for the first few weeks. As Tiffany and I bustled to leave for work at our clinics, most mornings Katie trailed us from room to room. Then, she took free rein in the house after we were gone—pillaging the cabinets for bags of snacks, scavenging anything left on the counters, rummaging through wastebaskets for paper and tissues, and leaving a trail of plundered goodies in her path. Upon our return, she greeted us as if we'd been abroad for weeks—whimpering and wildly bolting around the house in delirious fits, which Tiffany at some point dubbed "cracker dog." But, while certainly impassioned, these habits were not too surprising for a lively, curious young Labrador.

As fall led into winter, though, Katie's signs grew unmistakable. Each morning, she clung to our every movement, watching for any telltale clues that we'd be leaving soon—gathering our files, collecting our bags, brushing our teeth, and, over the weeks, even dressing. Her plundering while we were away transformed to sheer destruction. She splintered and shattered windowsills, scarred the front door with countless furrows, and troweled through our bedroom rug to the carpet pad beneath. And, when we came back home, at last, she greeted us with woeful eyes, baring her teeth in a sheepish smile and tucking her tail beneath her legs with only the tiniest wag. The smell of her fur and the scene behind her forecast what we could expect beyond. Dried in smudges on her coat and smeared in swaths across the rug, mingled with large soaked-up puddles of urine, lay sprawling trails of feces, further evidence of her anxiety while we were away.

Despite our understanding as vets, and our compassion for Katie's distress, we met with a range of emotions once home—anticipation, worry, and dread. Since we knew our dismay would just make things worse, we did our best to project utter calm as Tiff ushered Katie upstairs to the shower and I stayed downstairs to begin cleaning up. At times, though, it was all we could do to turn around, close the door, and take a few breaths, until we resigned ourselves to what lay ahead. Though, of course, we never scolded her, both of us choosing silence instead, our disappointment and frustration was never lost on Katie. Often, once she was clean from her shower, she slunk away to lie on her bed, while we tended to repairing the wreckage as quickly as we could. Yet, as soon as we were ready, she bounded gratefully into our arms, squirming and wriggling happily with irrepressible passion.

Dog owners often say to me that their dogs know when they've done something wrong, mistaking their dog's avoidance, downcast mug, and doleful eyes as evidence of regret. It would have been easy for us to agree, although as young vets we clearly knew better. Research proves that dogs' guilty looks are almost always in response to our human behavior, not because of their own misdeeds. Even in our silence, dogs notice the nuances of our reactions and heed all of our cues—overt and subtle.

Katie's destruction, certainly, was evidence of her anxiety. Her guilty looks were not admissions of misdeeds, but merely signals to ease our distress. Actions, indeed, speak louder than words, and Katie was forever mindful of ours. Signaling deference and appeasement, she quietly waited in the wings while we cleaned and scrubbed and, as we did so, worked through our emotions. And when we were ready to forgive, she always joined us willingly, having placed the woman down on the riverbank long before we did.

While I hold each of them closely in my heart, Katie and Maurice are not the exceptions, but simply examples of animals' steadfast willingness to forgive. Both, in their own way, honored relationship above circumstances and always stood ready to give as before. In a world where threats are real, joys are transient, and life itself is lived moment to moment, evolution favors animals' skillfulness at moving past their struggles to live in the present. Strife favors neither the individual nor the herd. Yet beyond their fitness for survival, animals demonstrate a capacity to *give as before* with grace and equanimity. With their steady constancy and abiding presence in our lives, they model how we, as humans, may endeavor to forgive.

9
Presence

There is one thing we can do, and the happiest people
are those who can do it to the limit of their ability. We
can be completely present. We can be all here. We can
give all our attention to the opportunity before us.

—Mark Van Doren

Though technically speaking, Murphy was a Christmas
puppy, nothing about him was a surprise. For months Ben
and Claire had each researched their favorite breeds and then
compared notes to narrow their choices. First Leonbergers,
next Dogues de Bordeaux, then otterhounds were dropped
from the list, till finally they were left with one. Then day
trips on the weekends followed—out to the Berkshires, down
to the Cape, and up to small towns in Vermont and New
Hampshire—visiting different bloodhound breeders, considering parents, looking at pups, being interviewed, then waiting. Everything about Murphy had been thoroughly planned
before he was born.

At first they'd intended on getting a puppy the summer
before Ben's third year at Brown. But they opted instead for

one last hurrah (before his caseload of patients grew larger and Claire began in earnest on her thesis for her MFA) when Claire's parents invited the couple to join them on vacation for their anniversary.

"We could get a puppy anytime," Claire explained as she recalled, "but an offer like that, for two weeks in Maui, was more than anyone could resist."

Then in September as classes resumed, with the prospect of winter soon looming ahead (not to mention the length of time Ben spent in clinics), they decided to call the breeder again.

"We hadn't planned on getting him, or any puppy, in time for Christmas, but then the idea . . . kinda grew on us." Claire would have three weeks on break, the breeder said the litter was huge (ten puppies could be seen on the X-ray, and possibly another one or two), and they adored both of the parents.

"At first, Claire really liked this one older pup—his name was Mackenzie—that came from the litter just before Murph."

"Yeah, he was cute," Claire recalled wistfully and then turned to Ben, "but we wanted a puppy. We both agreed"— she turned back to me—"you know, from the beginning."

The photos they showed of Murphy when he first came home at ten weeks old were as adorable as I'd expected. Even with his tiny frame amid that ample heap of wrinkles, I could almost see that familiar face of Trusty from *Lady and the Tramp*. Looking at him two years later, snuggled cozily on the rug, with Claire at one end, Ben at the other, and that ruffled jumble of fur between them, I couldn't help hearing somewhere back inside my head Trusty asking Lady and Jock, ". . . As my grandpappy Old Reliable used to say—don't recollect if I've ever mentioned Old Reliable before?"

With Murphy's head tucked next to Claire's thigh and one ear draped onto her lap, the folds and furrows around his eyes almost convinced me that he was dozing. But his nose assuredly gave him away, twitching and sniffing on full alert, true to his bloodhound heritage. I tried to imagine what he could be smelling. Perhaps the catnip or treats in my pack, despite the fact that both were almost hermetically sealed in plastic bags. Or maybe a whiff of moon bear or leopard clinging to my clothes since my morning visit to the zoo.

While watching Murphy, I started by asking, "So, when do you think the first episode was? You said in your history you can't quite remember."

Claire sighed, then answered, "It's been such a blur. They just seemed to suddenly start up from nowhere."

"I'd guess the first one was sometime in April," Ben offered.

"Really, you think so? That early?" Claire questioned. "I just don't think it's been long. I'm pretty sure it was the end of May."

Three months, I noted, as Claire recalled, "I'll never forget that first one, though."

Murphy and Claire were alone in the garden enjoying a bit of the afternoon sun after a day of classes apart and a couple of hours working at home on one of the sculptures for her thesis. Ben, of course, was still in clinics. Kate, their landlord, had just pulled past on the driveway between the main house and the cottage, and the girls, Bree and Emily, had hopped out of the car as soon as Kate had hit the brakes. Both were running toward the cottage—and wishfully out of earshot of Kate—to play with Murphy before their mother called them back to begin their homework. Emily was barely in the lead, laughing and racing ahead of Bree, trying to get to Murphy first.

"Wait a minute. It was definitely May. It was after school and really warm and the girls were still in their uniforms.

"Bree, I think, was waving a stick and calling Murphy to 'Come and get it' and keep her sister from reaching him first. And Murphy, I remember, stood next to me, looking back and forth at them. He was so confused which one to go to."

Claire paused a beat and then continued, "And that's when the ambulance went past—or maybe police car, I still don't know which—out on the street in front of the cottage. Whichever it was, the siren was loud (but not really louder than any other) and that's when Murphy just went . . . berserk.

"It was just so strange to watch it happen. One minute he's so happy and excited to see the girls again and the next minute he's attacking the bench—snapping and growling and snarling at it."

"And nothing like a siren had ever bothered him before, right?"

"No—never fazed him. And they go by . . . somewhat often—maybe, once or twice a week."

Nothing for two years. "Please, go on."

"Well, I remember jumping up and thinking, 'What just

happened? What's he attacking?' I wondered if a bee had just stung him. But he wasn't really acting hurt. And he'd never, ever acted that way anytime he'd been injured before. It was more like he was furious at something. He was grabbing the slats of the bench in his teeth and biting them so viciously that they were breaking and chunks of wood were literally falling from his mouth."

"So, what did you do?"

"I really didn't know what to do. I was pretty sure if I tried to stop him, I would just end up getting hurt. I know I shouted, 'Stay back!' to the girls, but they'd stopped cold as soon as it happened—I still feel bad, it must have been scary, even if both of them said they were fine—and they were far enough away that I wasn't really too worried for them. But still, to play it safe, I slowly slipped around the bench and pulled them back a little farther. And then the three of us just kinda stood there watching him. I know—that sounds pretty stupid, huh?"

"No, not really," I reassured her and then continued, "So, then what happened?"

"So, after another minute he finally stopped attacking the bench. And then he stood there—he looked exhausted—and panted and drooled and . . . that's about it."

"At what point did Murphy seem like he was himself again to you?"

"Well, for maybe like fifteen seconds, he just looked at the bench and seemed confused. That's when I began to wonder if maybe he'd had some type of seizure. His eyes seemed kind of glassy and dazed. And then . . . he turned and noticed us, and he got that Murphy look again. I thought it was over, whatever it was, but worried a little if it'd come back. So I sent the girls to go get Kate, grabbed my phone, and called our vet. We took him to the emergency clinic—Kate and the girls insisted on driving—and they checked him over, ran some tests, and kept him overnight to watch him."

The tests did not reveal a thing. His blood cell count and chemistry were in line with those for a two-year-old. With Murphy back to his same old self, Dr. Wellesley, their family vet, was at a loss to explain what had happened. The emergency doctor felt the same. So they left their diagnoses open—toxicity, metabolic disease, occult brain lesion, encephalitis, seizure disorder: The list went on. And, of course, they mentioned there was a chance it was some spontaneous form of aggression or another bizarre behavior. But with Murphy apparently back to himself, they opted to simply wait and see if anything happened and, if so, when.

They didn't wait long—only five days—before another incident. Like the first, it followed a siren, but this time they were on a walk. It was early Sunday morning, Ben was gratefully home from clinics, and the three of them were strolling through the neighborhood to the bakery. An ambulance passed with flashing lights but quietly, with no traffic that early, until it reached the intersection where Hope Street crosses Rochambeau. As soon as the siren began to blare, Ben and Claire saw Murphy jump, hastily scan the sidewalk around him, and frantically scramble across the path straight to the nearest telephone pole. As with the bench, he began to attack it savagely, with no holds barred, claws digging in, teeth bared and gnashing. This time Ben grabbed Murphy's leash, which Claire had been holding for most of the stroll, and tried to tug him away from the pole, although with close to a hundred pounds of ferocious bloodhound pulling back, Murphy clearly won the contest. Throwing caution to the wind, Claire meanwhile wrapped her arms around him in hopes that she might be able to calm him. Still unfazed by both of them, Murphy kept up his assault on the pole until he finally stopped, exhausted. The second time from start to finish lasted no more than two or three minutes, and after half a minute more, in which he tiredly panted and drooled, Murphy returned to his laid-back self.

Another occurred just two days later, but unlike the others, inside the cottage. Just before bedtime that Tuesday night, Claire was warming a cup of tea to help her relax before going to sleep. Murphy had already made his rounds outside in the garden an hour before and had gone ahead of Claire and Ben to claim his space on the featherbed. Nothing was out of the ordinary. There wasn't a siren or sound outdoors, at least that Ben or Claire could hear, and inside the cottage was blissfully quiet. Claire often made tea before going to sleep as part of her normal evening routine. But when the microwave finished heating and signaled to Claire that it was done as it always did with a series of beeps, Murphy charged in like a shot from the bedroom and lunged headlong straight at the oven. Although the microwave fared well, the kitchen pantry and Murphy did not. The good news was that it didn't last long—no more than two minutes of all-out aggression. But in that time, one cabinet door, three pantry shelves, a bowl, and a mug were damaged far beyond repair; Murphy fractured two incisors and scraped his gums till they were bleeding and raw.

After the third fit, when there was no siren, Ben and Claire to their dismay witnessed even more episodes, sometimes triggered by something new—the hair dryer, alarm clock, toaster oven, kitchen timer—as well as the old repeat offenders, but they rarely happened predictably. Most days nothing diverted Murphy from his happy-go-lucky self: Beeps, buzzes, squeaks, and sirens were viewed by Murphy indifferently.

"I really can't make sense of it," Ben suggested in med student mode. "A fire truck could roar on by with sirens blaring and Murph'll do nothing. And then on another day, a beep from my phone will send him into a full-blown fit."

Ben stood as he said, "Wait. Let me show you," while signaling for me to stay where I sat. "I'll be back in just a couple of seconds." He left us there. I heard a door open. And then, in a moment, Ben was back in the room holding an old wooden crate in his arms. "Here," he offered, "take a look at these," as he sat to join us back on the rug.

Inside the crate was a graveyard of victims: chewed-up alarm clocks; a demolished phone; what looked like an old cherished doll dismembered; a mangled iron (alarmingly it had been on at the time that Murphy grabbed it, and yet by some miracle he wasn't burned); a laptop computer so shattered I shuddered to look at it; a couple of gouged and bent candlesticks; and an assortment of shards from vases and mugs. The extent of the damage was truly impressive.

"And yet, through all of these incidents, neither of you has ever been injured?"

"Nope—never," Ben replied. "It doesn't matter what we do. Even when we try to stop him, he just stays focused on whatever he's attacking."

"Not even an accidental nip?"

"Well, sure, he's scratched me a couple of times when I've tried to hold him and he pushes away," Claire answered, "but, otherwise, that's really it."

"And do you do that very much?"

"What's that?" Ben asked.

"Try to hold him?"

"Sure, I've tried, but it doesn't really calm him down."

"Me too," Claire added, "though it never helps to comfort him. But I still keep thinking I should be trying, somehow, to help him stop and not just stupidly stand there and watch him." She paused, then added, "But also, if someone else is around, it's just . . . well, to be honest . . . embarrassing."

"Oh—I hear you—that doesn't help. But, no one else has been injured, right?"

"No, thank goodness. We couldn't live with ourselves."

"But, you gotta know," Ben stressed, "he's never come close to hurting anyone."

"It's like he avoids everyone that's near," Claire said, "except, of course, when we wrap ourselves around him. Even then, he pushes us away."

What are the odds? I wondered.

"Okay. Let's set aside, for a moment, the garden or out in the neighborhood. What do you do, if anything, when he has a fit right here at home? I mean, just looking in this crate, a laptop computer . . . the clocks . . . a phone? These things cost money, and you guys are students."

"Tell me about it," Ben mumbled. And then, more clearly, "But, it's not about the money. Claire and I both love this dog."

"He's like our kid. You understand." With a knowing glance, we read each other's eyes.

"So, we just grin and bear it," Ben explained with a wrinkled smile.

Claire cleared her throat and stroked Murphy's ears. "We've tried a few times to slip a toy in front of him—his fluffy monkey, which he totally adores; his squeaky bunny; a bone; a ball—so at least he's attacking something of his own, but nothing's ever really worked."

"And a couple of times we nudged him to the bathroom, once with a broomstick and the other with a folding chair," Ben offered. "I wanted to see what he'd do in the dark—if he'd get calm more quickly, or what." Then he sighed. "But that was a total disaster."

Both of them grinned.

"Oh, yeah," Claire added. "It was really bad. You wouldn't even believe the bathroom—shower curtain, cabinet doors, makeup, shampoo, bath salts. We won't be doing that again."

"I can only imagine," I replied. Claire's eyes met mine and her smile was contagious.

"I thought of taking pictures while Ben was cleaning up, but, well . . ."

I turned to flip through Murphy's medical records, to remind myself of all they had done in follow-up with Dr. Wellesley.

"And, of course, he's been worked up completely," I thought out loud as I scanned the reports. "Chemistries, UAs, CBCs, liver function and thyroid profiles, fasting blood glucose, a tox screen for lead, and a neuro consult with Dr. Danes." Then, looking back up to Ben and Claire, I said, "It looks like he put Murphy on potassium bromide and phenobarb, but not very long. Just a few weeks?"

"Yeah, all they did was make him dopey," Claire said. "The episodes didn't really change."

"He said he couldn't rule 'em out," Ben added, "but, he just didn't think we were dealing with seizures. So both vets said to come see you."

I'd seen the pattern from time to time but never in that particular breed, although that didn't really surprise me; since bloodhounds were uncommon in New England, I rarely saw one for any reason. But, of those dogs with similar signs, no two cases were quite the same. Each patient had their nuances: what sounds would trigger an episode, how they looked when they were aroused, where they directed their aggression, how long it took to calm back down, and what their families did with them during the fits and in between. For though in some respects their histories might seem similar, what caused the episodes varied from case to case.

We try so hard to piece together what science reveals

about the brain to better understand our patients—even more so with animals, who don't use words to explain their thoughts and feelings. Yet, in spite of all we understand from modern advances in medicine, much of what we see and treat still remains a mystery. Although two patients may seem much alike—one lunging from sirens, another from thunder, and both attacking whatever's nearby—what goes on inside their brains may differ and, likewise, so will how we care for them. Often what seems like a single disease is, in fact, a complex syndrome of different problems that look the same. So, in caring for our patients, we must be mindful of all we can learn from them, before their treatment and afterward. Practicing medicine becomes an art when we interweave what our patients can teach us with science, research, and our own experience, balancing knowledge with intuition.

With all this circling in my thoughts, I put a name to what Murphy faced: canine idiopathic aggression (a fancy way of saying that we weren't quite sure what caused his fits). For some dogs, such as Murphy, certain sounds may cause them pain for reasons that aren't really clear—perhaps their nerves or receptors for hearing acquire a sensitivity, although I've seen other patients where touches or smells can do the same. Some may have complex partial seizures of the temporal lobe or elsewhere in the brain, which can be hard to diagnose without recording an EEG during an actual episode. (Imagine a dog at the height of his aggression, electrodes connected to his head, with wires torn and flung in all directions.) For other dogs, whatever the trigger, their neurons may fire in a roundabout way through the brain's key emotional centers, provoking sometimes violent reactions to seemingly trivial stimuli. Still others may be driven by an all-consuming fear or panic with an overwhelming need to aggressively defend themselves.

Mulling over Murphy's case and considering what I'd seen and learned of him, my instincts knew which way to go. So as we sat and formed a plan, I listened to my intuition. "Weighing it all, in my opinion, these sounds are making Murphy very anxious, and that's provoking these fits of aggression."

"But I guess I don't really get it. Why would sounds like that make him anxious—and then only sometimes?" Claire asked while trying to sort it out.

"Well, I can give you all sorts of theories, but all I'd really be doing is guessing. And not knowing which is true, they don't really change what we should do. Trying to pinpoint what first happened that led our dog to develop a problem can sometimes be a booby prize. As much as we try to figure it out, we often end up at the very same question that the three of us face right now: 'So, where do we go from here?'"

In implementing a plan for Murphy, I began with practical management—ensuring Murphy's and everyone's safety, addressing sounds around the house, assessing when and where to take walks, and reinforcing his behavior at times when he was calm in the face of sounds that sometimes upset him. We added antianxiety meds based on my experience of seeing how essential they were in helping dogs with similar fits. And although the meds took a bit of tweaking, from sertraline to citalopram, and tuning the dosage so it was just right, within five to six months Murphy's signs had disappeared. He wasn't numb, dopey, sleepy, or less affectionate with Claire and Ben. To them, he seemed just the opposite—inquisitive, loving, playful, energetic—and they came to realize the toll his anxiety took in other ways well beyond the aggressive fits.

"I never realized how stressed he was, even before the episodes," Claire said one day in follow-up. "He never seemed anxious to either of us, when he was aggressive or otherwise. We thought he was just a quiet dog—of course, except for those wild fits. But, to see him now, he's just so much happier and . . . full of life. He's even tighter with Emily and Bree; as soon as they're home and he hears their voices, he's off like a shot to play with them. And you should see him in the neighborhood, sniffing around like he never did. It's hard to imagine he's the same dog that used to go crazy from all those sounds."

It's been five years since I last saw Murphy. Once Ben finished his internship and Claire completed her master's degree, they moved from Rhode Island to California for Ben to perform his residency, and then they settled in Laguna Beach. Through the years as we've kept in touch, Murphy's had a couple of bumps: just as they finished the drive out west and again before the baby was born. For both, the fits were mild and brief—only with sirens and quickly soothed, though he was a bit anxious in between. But the stretches were only for a couple of weeks and then he returned to his easygoing self. Though Murphy now is nine years old, he's as playful with their daughter, Nell, as he was with Bree and Emily. And while he's slowed a touch with age, he still enjoys his walks in the neighborhood and, most of all, along the shore, where he loves to sniff through the tidal pools and splash with Nell between the waves.

What's brought me back to think of Murphy so many times through all these years is not in the details of his case or even my fondness for him, Ben, and Claire. What touches me so deeply and keeps him so often in my thoughts is an image of him in the worst of his episodes. In those first few months as I worked with Murphy and we struggled with how best to care for him, I witnessed several aggressive fits, both out on the street and inside the cottage. Fraught with sudden anxiety that could be triggered at any time and compelled to cope as best he could, Murphy consistently turned away from people, particularly Ben and Claire, to focus on objects instead of them. Even when Ben and Claire interfered and could have been bitten, if only by accident, not once was either one of them injured. This wasn't just luck or coincidence but rather, I am certain, by Murphy's intention. In the height of his aggressive fits, he kept enough presence of body and mind to always ensure the safety of others. This is the image that stays with me still.

Presence is a state of being in which we focus our attention in the moment. It challenges us to accept what is happening as if we have chosen it intentionally. Even when we feel compelled or justified to resist what we're facing, being present involves working with circumstances instead of against them, or forgoing them. When we're fully present, we embrace each moment for all that it offers and then act accordingly.

In the story of "Three Questions," Leo Tolstoy tells the tale of a king who wondered how he could best rule his kingdom. In doing so, he asked three questions: When is the right time to begin? Whom should he listen to and whom should he avoid, especially when facing critical decisions? And, at any given moment, what is the most important thing to do? The king knew if he answered these, his kingdom would prosper as long as he ruled.

For months he pondered and brooded and struggled till, at last, the king sent out a decree that he would bestow a great reward to anyone throughout the land who could teach him the answers to these questions. So, wise men came from near and far, seeking audience with the king to offer him what he desired, but each one answered differently.

As they responded to the first question, "When is the right time to begin?" some advised he draft a schedule, planning his life ahead by years and, once completed, must live by it. Others proclaimed that this was absurd—that no one could plan for every deed; instead, they told him to stay alert, hour by hour, minute by minute, setting aside all other distractions, and then do what each moment required. A few declared no single man could know the best time to begin and suggested the king assemble a cabinet of wise men to tell him when he should act. Still others insisted that such a council would only muddy the waters and make his decisions more difficult. They claimed the king should consult a magician to learn beforehand what best to do.

Their answers to the second question varied as much as

with the first. Some told him he must trust his legal advisers. Several suggested that doctors knew best. Many thought priests and ministers were wisest, while others argued a king should trust his warriors above everyone else.

As for the question of what to do, a few reminded the king that he could always depend on his skills at warfare. Some professed science was the highest pursuit. And others avowed religious worship.

With the scholars giving such different answers, the king felt he could agree with none and sent them away without reward.

Now more unsettled from all he had heard, the king set out with his bodyguard on a quest to find the answers himself. One day while the two men wandered through a village, the townsfolk told the king about a monk who lived deep in the woods and was highly revered for the wisdom he offered. And still not having found the answer to his questions, the king set out in search of this holy man. He traveled for days to the edge of the kingdom, through lonely valleys and rolling hills, till he reached the forest where the recluse lived. Then, leaving his horse and escort behind to wait for him by the trailside, he changed from his gowns into commoner's clothes, and set off on the path through the forest alone.

The trail climbed quickly and steeply upward, with snow-clad peaks towering overhead, till at last it led to a simple hut in a narrow clearing—really no more than a gap in the forest—not far below the first mountain crest. Just across that small, rock-strewn meadow, the king found the holy man, shovel in hand, outside his cottage tilling a garden. He was frail and older than the king had supposed, and with each strike of the monk's spade to the ground, the king could hear his straining breath.

Pausing a moment as the king approached, the old man looked up to say, "Hello," and then bent down to continue his work.

The king replied, "Greetings," as he came closer, then began telling his story while the monk tilled the earth—the journey he'd been on, why he had come, and the questions he'd struggled for so long to answer.

Leaning his body now and then on his shovel, the old man listened thoughtfully, furrowed his brow with concentration, and nodded from time to time, but, once the king finished, he went back to his digging without as much as a single word.

Concerned that he might just have overwhelmed the hermit, or that perhaps the old man was too tired to talk, the king offered: "Excuse me. If you're willing, could I help you? I can work in the garden while you rest awhile."

With a good-hearted smile, the monk replied, "Thank you," as he reached out and passed the shovel to the king. And turning, he walked to some steps outside the cottage, dipped an old cup in a bucket of water, and wiped his brow with a towel that lay next to it. Then he sat down to rest and watch.

The monk sat in silence and the king toiled without a word, trusting his questions would be answered in due time. But, after digging two full beds, from one end of the plot to the other, he paused and called out to the monk, "I was wondering, now that you've rested a bit, if you had thought about the answers to my questions."

The old man looked back with that smile once again as he seemed to consider the king's question for a bit. Then he stood and returned to the king's side in the garden.

"Now it is your turn to rest and let me do my work again."

The king, though, refused to return the spade. Instead, he simply resumed his digging. After several moments more, the old man turned and walked out of the garden, back to his post on the steps once again.

An hour passed, and then another, and still the king continued to dig until the sun slipped below the treetops and steeped the sky with vermillion hues. At last the king stuck the spade to the ground, looked back to where the holy man sat, and crossed through the rows of freshly tilled earth to him.

"As much as I've been willing to help, I came here today in search of answers. Yet, in spite of my work, I'm no more the wiser. If you can offer me no advice, then perhaps it is time I resume my journey."

"Wait! Look behind you," the hermit interrupted. "Here comes someone running." And then he suggested, "Let us see who it is."

The king turned around and saw a stranger, a bearded man, running toward them from the woods. Even from a distance, he could see the man was wounded. He held his arms against his sides and clenched his belly with his hands; yet, blood had clearly seeped from beneath and soaked his shirt a dark crimson. Just as the injured man reached the king, he stumbled to the ground and fainted.

Both the king and hermit rushed to his side, while the stranger lay there in a stupor moaning. Working together to loosen his clothes, they quickly found the wellspring of his blood—a deep gash in his abdomen. Quickly with a handkerchief and then a towel the old man gave him, the king plugged the wound as best he could, but the blood did not stop seeping through. Again and again he removed the towel, wrung the blood out with his hands, and pressed it back onto the wound until the bleeding finally stopped. Then, with a fresh towel the monk had brought, the king wrapped the wounded man's belly once more.

It wasn't long before the man awoke—though not quite lucid in his thoughts—and between incomprehensible words, begged for a sip of water. Silently the monk arose, walked through the garden to a nearby well, and returned with a fresh bucket of water, which the king then offered in sips to the stranger.

The sun had set and the air was getting colder, so the king and the monk lifted the wounded man and, with him cradled in their arms, carried him to the old monk's bed. Weakly thanking both of them, the man closed his eyes and rested quietly. Tucked underneath a woolen blanket and nestled in the warmth of the hut, the man woke just enough to thank them both, and then dropped back into a fitful sleep.

The king, exhausted from his journey and all his work since he'd arrived, sat down at last in the threshold to the hut. Gazing across the long rows in the garden and on past the meadow at the darkening skies, the king soon drifted off in the doorway and slept on the floor there all through the night.

When the king awoke the following morning, he wasn't sure at first where he was. Then, as his memory came back to him, he turned his gaze to the wounded stranger. The bearded man lay awake on the bed, studying him with a smile on his face.

In a weak voice, the man begged softly, "Please, forgive me," to the king.

"But, I don't know you," the king replied, "and have nothing to forgive you for."

"That may be true, but I know you," the wounded man confessed to the king, "for I have been your enemy, sworn to avenge my brother's execution and your seizure of my property. I stalked you as you searched for the hermit and resolved to kill you right here in these woods. But, while I lay in wait for you, your bodyguard discovered me and wounded me as I escaped. Had you and the old man not dressed my wounds, I surely would have bled to death."

He paused a moment and then continued, "I sought to kill you, and you saved my life. Now, if I live, and if you wish it, I will work as your faithful servant and bid my sons to do the same. Again, I beg that you forgive me."

The king was stunned to hear the man's story as well as the plans to ambush him while he wandered through the woods alone. But, as he reflected on what could have happened, he also surprisingly felt relieved, for the man had resolved to assassinate him and quite possibly could have succeeded. And preferring to have an avid ally in place of a fervent enemy, the king forgave the man graciously and resolved to restore his property.

Taking leave of the wounded man, the king walked outside to look for the monk and found him once again in his garden, this time sowing seeds in the rows. "I think it's time I say my good-byes," the king said, standing next to him. "But before I leave, I wondered if I might ask one last time for your answers to my questions."

The monk, still kneeling, looked up at the king and claimed, "But you already have been answered."

"Answered—how? What do you mean?" the king asked, confused, looking down at the monk.

"Do you not see?" replied the old hermit. "If you had not pitied me in my weakness and dug these beds for me yesterday, that man inside would surely have attacked you, and you would have regretted not staying here with me. So yesterday, when you were digging, that was the most important time, I was the most important man, and doing me good was your most important business. Indeed, you stand here because of your choices.

"Later that day, when the wounded man stepped from the woods into this meadow, the most important time was when you tended to his wounds, he was the most important person, and your caring for him is what mattered most.

"The answers to your questions," he offered, "have always been in front of you. *Now* is the one time that is important. This present moment is the only time for which you have any choice or power. The person whom to listen to is the person who stands before you now, for you can never know for certain when you will be with another. And what should you do above all else? Do that other person good, for that alone is why we are sent into this life."

The story, of course, is a metaphor for the questions we face in every moment. We are the king, and our lives are the journey. The monk is the wisdom we hold deep in ourselves. The wounded man is our adversities, and we choose in each moment how we wish to deal with him. If we ignore the wounded man and leave him to die as he comes before us, we lose an opportunity for growth and self-discovery. And then that opportunity is gone. If we resist him, the risk is the same, but we shift our focus to the struggle, missing what else the moment offers. But if, instead, we choose, as the king did, to embrace the man and learn from him, we open our lives to new possibilities. And our experience in that moment is richer.

Whenever my thoughts take me back to Murphy, I marvel at how he was always present. Engulfed with anxiety and compelled to react, he did not try to resist his aggression, but instead with intention worked through it, to always ensure that others were safe. And so, he directed his fits at objects.

Murphy's resolve was exceptional. But where he focused is not unique. Animals, by their very nature, fully live in the present moment. Clearly, they remember the past, and certainly they anticipate the future. But they—unlike us—do not dwell on them. A springbok gazelle at a watering hole, while drinking along with the rest of the herd, does not stop to ponder his reflection, thinking back to the good old days when he was a younger, more virile buck. While lost in thought about his past, he could easily end up instead as prey. Likewise, the cheetah that's stalking him does not then worry where he'll find his next meal when the buck starts pronking to warn the herd that he is near. Both predator and prey are fully present in the moment, aware of other animals, themselves, and their environment.

Now and then at the end of the day while driving home, I find myself turning down our street with no recollection of the last few miles. It's unsettling as the driver. *Where was I? What did I miss? What other cars were on the road? Did I stop at the stop sign? Which route did I take?*

My daughter asks, "Can we do it after homework?"

"Huh?" I jump back from my thoughts. "Do what?"

What was I thinking?

Whether because of the pace of our lives, the reasoning power of our human brains, or the simple indulgence of dwelling on ourselves—our hopes and wishes, worries and fears, concerns, frustrations, priorities—we live so much of our lives lost in thought: reflecting on the past, dwelling on the future, or thinking of some time other than the moment, some place other than where we are right now. But we do so at a costly price. We miss what is right in front of us. We don't even notice the wounded man or, if we do, we choose to ignore him or even fight to be rid of him. And unlike the king, we don't ask the monk, even as he softly reminds us to notice.

Early this morning, while at the zoo and making my

rounds with a couple of keepers, I looked through the trees in search of the leopards and found them perched high up in the rocks, Jakarta on one and Surabaya on another. And though both appeared as if they were dozing, I knew quite well that they were not. A flick of his ear; a twitch of her tail; through his half-shut eyes, a glint of recognition—all told me that they were fully aware, tracking our movements and our hushed conversation first through one window, then the next.

While watching them, it occurred to me that I hadn't heard what their keeper, Ted, had said for . . . *how long? Half a minute? Maybe more?* I tried to catch up on the conversation by joining the pieces into a phrase—"growling . . . chunk meat . . . her first . . . rolling"—but try as I might, their meaning escaped me.

I confessed, "I'm sorry. I lost what you were saying."

Ted chuckled. "No worries—that's okay. You thinking about the meeting this morning?"

"Nah—not really. I was watching them."

And I was reminded once again how much I look to animals to keep me in the moment. For though I was present with the leopards, absorbed in ministering to their needs, I also was lost to someone right beside me: another moment, another person, another opportunity.

Perhaps we're conditioned to tune out what's in front of us—so many faces, so much information, so many choices; perhaps it's all too much. Maybe it's just the pace of our lives. Or, possibly, we look past each other, lost in our own private world of thoughts. Yet, when we look at animals, they vividly reflect their presence in the moment.

And that reflection can serve us well. When we fail to hear the monk, the animals around us offer a bridge from our thoughts back to the present—a reminder, an embodiment of three questions we should ask ourselves: *When is the right time to begin? Whom should we listen to? What should we do now?*

10

What Lies Beneath

*A human being is a part of the whole called by
us "Universe," a part limited in time and space. He
experiences himself, his thoughts and feelings as
something separated from the rest—a kind of
optical delusion of his consciousness. This delusion
is a kind of prison for us, restricting us to our personal
desires and to affection for a few persons nearest to us.
Our task must be to free ourselves from this prison by
widening our circle of compassion to embrace all
living creatures and the whole of nature
in its beauty.*
—Albert Einstein

As I write this final chapter, it's summertime in New England. School is out and our mornings start earlier, compared with the regular school year routine—swim team at seven thirty, camp at nine o'clock, and breakfast gobbled down sometime in between. On the drive from the pool to camp, I peek through the windows of other cars—a menagerie of humans rushing in different directions to get wherever we're headed to next. I catch a glimpse of the other faces, as we move along in different lanes or cross paths at intersections, to remind myself real people surround us. It almost seems to come naturally, that we narrow our focus to our own lives.

A thunderstorm had been predicted and it's hit just at the end of swim practice. In a rush of water, the streets are flooded.

"It looked like you guys practiced racing dives before you finished," I say to my daughter.

"Uh-huh," she replies between bites of her bagel, "but then the coach, at the very end, let us jump off the diving board. The other lanes didn't have time—"

A dot in the road catches my attention. Somewhere a familiar form registers in my mind: a pair of black dots, a thin strip at the end, an off-brown rounded shape curled in between. Huddled dead center in the middle of the road, a field mouse has lost his way, caught in the torrent of rain and thunder. Lost on all sides to broad sheets of flowing water, he's surrendered to the sudden storm. I think of braking— *not a chance, not safe*—and decide in that second to swerve instead. I steel myself as I look back in the mirror. The mouse hasn't moved an inch. I cringe to imagine how long he'll survive.

"Did you see that?"

"What?"

"There's a mouse in the road. I'm pretty sure he's still alive."

"Oh, where? I don't see him."

"Wait, I'll show you in just a sec. We're going to pull around again. I feel like we need to try to help him, sweetie."

I scan the road to either side. By chance, to our good luck (or his), there's a break in the traffic just at that moment, and the next car coming is a good stretch away. Quickly turning, we circle around and come to a stop in front of him. I squint through the window. He hasn't budged. For a moment, I wonder if he's alive. But then I notice a blink of his eyes. *Or is that just my imagination?*

I turn on our flashers as cars approach behind us. "It looks like they're stopping. Okay, here goes."

I brace myself, open the door, and in only seconds, I'm as soaked as the mouse. I quickly slip over to the passenger side and wave for the drivers of the cars to pass us by. A line has formed behind the first, and as he pulls forward the others follow. One, then another, and another, and on.

Now that they're moving, they're barely even slowing. While I stand and wait for the line to end, I keep checking on the mouse to see if he has moved. Out in the downpour and a few feet away, it's easy to see that he's still alive. Yet, remarkably, he's staying put, in spite of the noise of the cars whizzing past and the waves of water they leave in their wake.

Two minutes. Three minutes. *Do that many people really drive this way?* And though I already know the answer, somehow I still feel surprised. Usually, I'm just one of many, in a steady stream of all kinds of humans, passing through on their daily routine.

I recognize a logo on a door. Our gardener, Jeff, pulls up in his truck and rolls down his window to offer us help. His brother and another worker sit beside him in the cab. In spite of myself, I feel my cheeks blush and point to the tiny, wet lump in the road.

"You know me—that crazy vet. It's a mouse. I had to try to help him. Hey, thanks, though, for stopping to check."

Jeff looks at me with a knowing smile then continues on in the pouring rain with a line of cars, once again, behind him. As I wait for the traffic to ease for a moment—just a few seconds when the road is clear—two more huddled shapes catch my eye. I blink, unbelieving, but they're still there. A pair of skunks, also caught in the storm, are curled into black-and-white mounds in the gutter. With drains overflowing, a river surrounds them. And though their coats are as drenched as my clothes, I can make out their faces surprisingly well and see that they're utterly overwhelmed.

A car races past from the other direction, hits a swollen puddle of rain, and douses me thickly from head to toe. As soaked as I was, I feel even wetter. With a sigh and a chuckle of disbelief, I peer in the window to see if my daughter is smiling back, but the rain is coming down much too hard.

A break in the traffic—the road is empty. Quickly, I crouch down next to the mouse—far too bewildered to respond to the shadow that now is bending over him—and easily pick him up by the tail. Instincts on, he wriggles and squirms, legs stretched out in all directions, reaching with his paws to grasp onto anything. I block the picture in my mind of how I imagine we must look—both of us waterlogged, captor and prey—and, with him dangling in my hands, quickly jog across the road and onto a soggy stretch of lawn. For just a few heartbeats (more of his than mine), we pause in that moment to consider each other—a world apart in perspective and experience, yet now our lives are assuredly linked. And then, with a blink, he scurries off between the bushes.

As I trudge back through the swamp of rain-soaked grass, I look to the gutter to check on the skunks. Both have shifted a bit from the road to be far enough from the passing cars that I trust their instincts are keeping them safe, despite the river that still surrounds them.

I stop to open the passenger door, expecting to see my daughter's smile at seeing her father so thoroughly soaked, and to point out the skunks, since I'm not sure she saw them. With flushed cheeks and reddened eyes, she quickly rubs a tear with her sleeve. My *sensitive daughter—so much like her father*.

"Oh, sweetie, no worries. Everything's fine."

She smiles and softly says, "I know."

"He scurried away into the bushes. But, hey, did you get to see the skunks?"

She hadn't. So, I point them out, and together we watch them for a minute. Still a safe distance from the road, they've shifted to huddle more closely together. Cars whir past and the rain drives harder.

"We better get going," I tell my daughter. "I'll check them again on my way back to town." I dash back around to the driver's side, wait for our turn, then pull into the traffic, once more just another in a steady passing stream of cars.

The animals with whom we share our lives—the vizsla we adopted when the kids were little; a border collie raised since birth to help a herdsman tend his flock; the hyacinth macaw our best friend bought while still in college and who has kept her company through all these years—we hold in our hearts with loving affection. The wild animals we see at zoos—a lion surveying his domain from a nearby hill as we pass him on safari; a bask of crocodiles fixedly staring with jagged-tooth smiles while sunning on the riverbank; a recent litter of bat-eared fox kits who, in their playful behaviors and antics, remind us of our dogs at home—all draw us in with a mystic allure. Even a field mouse lost on the road or a pair of wet skunks huddled in a gutter, caught in the downpour of a summer thunderstorm, can spark our sense of connectedness, if we allow ourselves to notice them.

Across a remarkably wide range of species, from blue-crowned conures to lowland gorillas, northern sea otters, and spectacled bears, animals tap into human emotions in ways that other people cannot—even those who are closest to us. They enchant us, seduce us, and help us to laugh. They inspire our visions, give us pause, and fill us with a sense of wonder and awe. They reach into our very hearts to touch us in ways we don't understand, stirring us to heights of joy as well as heartrending depths of sorrow.

In the opening pages of this book, we considered a fundamental question: *Why are we so drawn to animals?* Common history, memories from childhood, compassion, empathy, longing for connection, our willingness to be vulnerable, a feeling of acceptance without judgment or rejection—all play a role in what attracts us to them. Beyond all of these, the traits that we share—sensitivity, integrity, presence, forgiveness, and each of the others we've considered in these chapters, are not only part of our bond with them but also add to their allure.

Yet, from all I've seen and heard through the years as I've worked hand in hand with clients and patients, I am certain what draws us together goes deeper. I believe our sense of kinship with animals comes from our souls connecting with theirs. And though this may be contentious to some, I'm far from alone in believing so. From Hippocrates and Pythagoras to Martin Luther and Pope John Paul II, since the earliest roots of Western culture (and almost certainly well before then), countless luminaries, philosophers, clergymen, and common folk have held this to be an essential truth.

This conviction that animals have souls like ours can be traced to the roots of the word *animalis*, which, literally, in Latin means "having a soul." To ancient scholars, the *anima*, or soul, was the spirit of life found in creatures and humans that makes up our essential nature. And how our predecessors viewed the soul is not unlike how we do now.

The most recent version of the *Oxford English Dictionary* defines the soul as the "spiritual or immaterial part of a human being or animal, regarded as immortal." The soul is the seat where our spirit resides. Yet, though it's within us, it survives our death, for it's not in our bodies or physical features. The soul is the essence of who we are and holds those traits that make us unique: our character, emotions, identity, and spirit.

In the stories of the animals in this book, I've sought to portray what I perceived of their souls: the nature of their characters, the emotions through which they endured, how they expressed themselves, their uniqueness in identity, and a sense of the spirit that filled their lives. Though it may seem beyond the scope of traditional behavioral medicine, I believe I should consider these traits of animals' souls as I care for them.

Now and then I think back to that day when Jen told me Baxter had passed. As we sat on the phone sharing memories of him, we cried not so much for the void that he left as for the ways he had touched our hearts through all those years he was alive. What we both missed of Baxter was his calm and loving nature; his untiring passion for retrieving paper balls; how completely accepting he was of his fate—the pains that he suffered from FHS, Jen's school and work schedules, his different homes—how lovingly he cared for Jen (on a quiet evening or in the midst of a fit, his greatest comfort was being with her); and their favorite way to spend time together: out on the deck, while Jen sat and read and Baxter slyly stalked squirrels and birds (though not quite concealed) from his grassy lair. For what touched us both was Baxter's spirit. Without a doubt, our souls connected with his.

With Sakari, as I sat in that cave at the zoo, pondering her fate visit after visit, what stirred my heart so deeply was the ghost that lay perched in her tree. Long before the first time I saw her, Sakari's spirit left the leopard in that pen.

What remained there was only a shell—a body with no will to live, no reason to do so, empty and spent. The ache I felt that haunts me still is for the leopard I never knew. *Where did her spirit go? What was she like before it was gone? Why couldn't I find a way—any way—to bring her back?*

Over the years from time to time, I've seen other animals like Sakari, shadows of beings who, in the course of their lives, have somehow surrendered their spirits. As I struggle to care for them, something, I sense, is palpably different from what I find with other animals. With them, it feels as if I'm working alone, trying desperately to open a door beyond which lies a cold, vacant house. As much as I try to reach out to them, all that remains is a haunting absence. There is no soul left for mine to meet.

Each of the animals we've considered in these pages—Pandora and Persephone with their nighttime games; Maurice's reclusive avoidance of Jacques, when his brother started attacking him; Dougal with his penchant for reflections; Murphy and his steadfast presence during all his episodes; Sabrina in her acceptance of Mia—impressed me far beyond the details of their cases. In truth, what I remember most was simply by offering care to them, I felt touched in some way by their spirits.

The belief that animals' souls touch ours is a widely held principle that crosses many cultures. Here in North America, near the turn of the twentieth century, Chief Letakots-Lesa of the Native American Pawnee tribe spoke of this relationship between animals' souls and ours:

In the beginning of all things, wisdom and knowledge were with the animals, for Tirawa, the One Above, did not speak directly to man. He sent certain animals to tell men that he showed himself through the beasts, and that from them, and from the stars and the sun and the moon should man learn. . . . When man sought to know how he should live, he went into solitude and cried until in vision some animal brought wisdom to him. It was Tirawa, in truth, who sent his message through the animal. He never spoke to man himself, but gave his command to beast or bird, and this one came to some chosen man and taught him holy things.

I believe each of us is the holy man on our own journey, crying somewhere deep inside, yearning to feel more connected to others—animals and people—and the greater world in which we live. And surrounding every one of us are animals ready to serve as teachers by opening doors to new perspectives and ways of being beyond how we live. All we really need to do is pause a moment to notice them—in our homes and backyards, at the park and the zoo, or even along the side of the road—and take the time to truly watch and listen, setting aside the pace of our day, our thoughts about the past and future, and our countless wishes, worries, and fears that distract us so much from that precious moment.

If we are willing to focus on animals, putting aside ourselves for a bit, Tirawa can teach us holy things, for animals offer us ways of being that we cannot find simply by ourselves. And in that moment, if we allow our souls to touch those of animals, together we can change how we live from day to day, and discover a deeper sense of connection to others and the world around us.

Acknowledgments

Giving myself the time and space to step from the world of working with animals and fully into the shoes of a writer has been a dream of mine for more than a decade and a labor of love for half of that. In the course of my doing so, there have been many who have helped me along the way, gently nudged me, held my hand, and inspired me to stay true to the vision I've held for these pages and my hopes for how they will touch others' lives. It has been a truly remarkable journey, though one that I feel has just begun.

To my agent, Rebecca Gradinger, I offer my deepest gratitude for seeing the worth in a small spark of writing, holding the vision to see it through, and guiding me in each of the steps—so many more than I ever imagined—through which I've traveled along the way.

I've often wondered through the years, while reading authors' acknowledgments, about the relationship between writers and their editors. So many, it seems, share a special bond that is born from the book on which they've worked together. I am forever grateful to my editor, Vanessa Mobley, for so very much—the wisdom and insights she poured into this project, her steadfast support while I wrote and rewrote, her encouragement and belief in me as a writer, and her car-

214

ing attention toward shaping this book into all it could be. I consider it an honor and a privilege to have worked with her.

To the truly exceptional team at the Crown Publishing Group, I am profoundly grateful for all the hard work, commitment, and care they have invested in this book. I offer my heartfelt gratitude to Molly Stern, our publisher; Sheila O'Shea, our Broadway publisher; Penny Simon, our publicist; and Miriam Chotiner-Gardner for always being there. To Eric White, who designed the cover, and Songhee Kim, who designed the inside pages, thank you. To Annsley Rosner, Jay Sones, Tricia Wygal, Danielle Crabtree, and Claire Potter, I also offer my thanks.

From the moment I met Sandi Mendelson, I instinctively knew I belonged in her hands for sharing my vision with the rest of the world. To Sandi, especially, as well as her team—Claire Daniel, Deborah Jensen, and all at Hilsinger-Mendelson—I am so very grateful for their passion with this project.

I spent two winters writing much of this book while in fellowships at the MacDowell Colony. Working all day long without distraction in my studio, being served exquisite meals made with tender, loving care, and sharing the company of so many amazingly talented artists was a privilege and gift. My thanks to the remarkable group of people at MacDowell who make it all happen, with special thanks to Blake Tewksbury, who always brought just the right touch to each day.

I will always be so very grateful to Charlie Nakamura for those life-altering talks we shared in Hilo and Kona and all those places we'd stop in between, to Eric Johnson for his sage advice while we drove on the back roads of Oahu and Kauai and for our early mornings when we'd talk story while eating breakfast at the Yum Yum Tree, and to Carl Izumi for his good-natured kindness on my trips to Maui, including that night we found ourselves locked behind the gates at the KKGC. My deepest thanks to each of them for their friendship through all the years.

Though in some ways my residency seems ancient history, I believe my memories from Cornell will never fade. I am forever grateful to Katherine Houpt for taking me under her wing and bringing me into the world of behavioral medicine. From all the time she invested teaching me in clinics, at rounds, and in the field, the greatest gift she gave me was her abiding encouragement to think on my own and decide for myself, outside the box of current doctrine and theories. She was my guide and mentor then and to this day is a trusted friend.

I wish to thank David Wirth, Lyle George, Richard Freedland, and Noel Laing—all men whose footsteps I tremendously respect. Each inspired me to dare to reach to my highest aspirations and left an enduring impression on me. I am thankful for each of them being in my life.

I am forever grateful to Kris King, Noni Allerdice, and Johanna Mitchell—enduring friends through so many years since my "monk" days back in Oregon. Whether a short drive away or across the country, they have been there anytime I needed to offer me insight, compassion, and love. I treasure each of these remarkable women for who they are and what they do in the world.

I'd like to give special thanks to Meg Stowe for her keen eye, insightful perspective, and remarkable gift as a visionary. She's been a confidant, advisor, and a trusted friend along with Jeremy, her husband, as together we've watched our daughters grow.

To Sara Granoff-Schor and Charlie Schor I offer my thanks for sharing their hearts, their open arms, and their kitchen table. They've made me laugh and touched my heart in more ways than they'll even know.

To Nancy Yielding and Lisa Tener, my thanks for coaching me as I learned to be a writer. To our team at Veterinary Healing Arts, I am so very grateful for their care, support, and laughter.

My thanks to Joe Fallon for sharing such wonderful stories of Catie. And, of course, special thanks to Catie, herself.

To the countless animals I've known through the years, I am profoundly grateful for their presence in my life and the lessons they have offered me. Though my gratitude in words may not be so important, I hope that, in some way, I've touched their lives in return for the many ways they've deeply touched mine. My thanks, especially, to our dear cats, Fritz and Clara, and our selflessly loving dogs, Corrigan and Katie.

As I stepped into the shoes of a writer, I hadn't really fathomed how much my life would change—the countless hours I'd spend alone lost in my thoughts, the struggles and frustrations, the immeasurable highs, the depth of fulfillment I'd find along the way. It's a journey which I've come to love. And through it all, my greatest thanks are to my wife and my daughter for the countless ways they've been there for me constantly with patience, understanding, and love.

To Giselle, you are my brightest star, my greatest inspiration.

To Tiffany, my soul mate, you're the essence of all that is good in my life.

Notes

Introduction

1 **Lots of people talk to animals:** Benjamin Hoff, *The Tao of Pooh* (New York: Penguin, 1982), 29.

Chapter One: Connection

9 **If all the beasts were gone:** Ted Perry, film script for *Home* (produced by Southern Baptist Radio and Television Commission, 1972), reprinted in Rudolf Kaise, "Chief Seattle's Speech(es): American Origins and European Reception," in *Recovering the Word: Essays on Native American Literature*, ed. Brian Swan and Arnold Krupat (Berkeley: University of California Press, 1987), 525–30.

16 **one-half to two-thirds of us:** *U.S. Pet Ownership & Demographics Sourcebook Key Findings* (Schaumburg, Ill.: Center for Information Management, American Veterinary Medical Association, 2007), 1–2; *Gauging Family Intimacy: A Social Trends Report* (Washington, D.C.: Pew Research Center, 2006), 1.

16 **And more than 90 percent affirm:** *Pet Owner Survey* (Milton: Ontario Veterinary Medical Association, 2007).

16 **almost half of us confess:** *AAHA Pet Owners Survey* (Lakewood, Colo.: American Animal Hospital Association, 2004).

Chapter Two: Sensitivity

26 **One often hears of a horse:** William Butler Yeats, *The Cutting of an Agate* (New York: Macmillan, 1912), 17.

Chapter Three: Mindfulness

47 **When I lost my way:** From a conversation between Napoléon Bonaparte and Barry Edward O'Meara, his physician, noted in A. Cunningham, *Anecdotes of Napoleon Bonaparte and His Time, Compiled from Every Authentic Source* (Philadelphia: John B. Perry, 1855), 14.

56 **Penfield plotted out the first:** Wilder Penfield, *No Man Alone: A Neurosurgeon's Life* (Boston: Little, Brown, 1977), 207–21.

Chapter Four: Responsiveness

59 **"The conventional theory of the brain":** C. H. Vanderwolf, *The Evolving Brain: The Mind and Neural Control of Behavior* (New York: Springer Science, 2007), 16.

67 **According to recognized aerotechnical tests:** "Igor Sikorsky: The Aviation Pioneer Speaks," Igor Sikorsky Historical Archives, http://www.sikorskyarchives.com/.

70 **hundreds of thousands of cats were hunted:** Adele Conover, "Not a Lot of Ocelots," *Smithsonian Magazine*, June 2002, 64–68.

70 **as many as nine in a single year:** Laura Tangley, "Cat on the Spot," *National Wildlife*, April–May 2006, 31–37.

Chapter Five: Expressivity

91 **Man himself cannot express love:** Charles Darwin, *The Expression of the Emotions in Man and Animals* (New York: D. Appleton, 1886), 11.

93 **with those of prehistoric wolves:** Stanley J. Olsen and

John W. Olsen, "The Chinese Wolf, Ancestor of New World Dogs," *Science* 197 (1977): 533–35.

93 **they likely shared a common shelter:** Carles Vilà, Peter Savolainen, Jesús Maldonado, Isabel R. Amorim, John E. Rice, Rodney L. Honeycutt, Keith A. Crandall, Joakim Lundeberg, and Robert K. Wayne, "Multiple and Ancient Origins of the Domestic Dog," *Science* 276 (1997): 1687–89.

94 **"Take a dozen railroad whistles":** Emily C. Blackman, *History of Susquehanna County, Pennsylvania: From a Period Preceding Its Settlement to Recent Times* (Philadelphia: Claxton, Remsen, & Haffelfinger, 1873), 281.

96 **the concept of an alpha wolf:** L. David Mech, "Whatever Happened to the Term 'Alpha Wolf'?" *International Wolf* 18 (2008): 4–8.

99 **not supported by the group:** David W. MacDonald and Geoff M. Carr, "Variation in Dog Society: Between Resource Dispersion and Social Flux," in *The Domestic Dog: Its Evolution, Behaviour, and Interactions with People*, ed. James Serpell (Cambridge: Cambridge University Press, 1995), 199–216.

104 **For words, like Nature, half reveal:** Alfred, Lord Tennyson, *In Memoriam* (London: Edward Moxon, 1850), 5.

105 **Extensive research with human beings:** Starkey Duncan, "Nonverbal Communication," *Psychological Bulletin* 72 (1969): 118–37; Albert Mehrabian and Susan R. Ferris, "Inference of Attitudes from Nonverbal Communication in Two Channels," *Journal of Consulting Psychology* 31 (1967): 248–52; Albert Mehrabian, "Significance of Posture and Position in the Communication of Attitude and Status Relationships," *Psychological Bulletin* 71 (1969): 359–72; Stanley E. Jones and Curtis D. LeBaron, "Research on the Relationship Between Verbal and Nonverbal Communication: Emerging Integrations," *Journal of Communication* 52 (2002): 499–521; Dacher Keltner and Paul Ekman, "Facial Expression of Emotion," in *Handbook of Emo-*

tions, 2nd ed., ed. Michael Lewis and Jeanette M. Haviland-Jones (New York: Guilford Publications, 2000), 236–49.

105 **we pick up on nonverbal cues:** Janine Willis and Alexander Todorov, "First Impressions: Making Up Your Mind After 100-ms Exposure to a Face," *Psychological Science* 17 (2006): 592–98; Joel S. Winston, Bryan A. Strange, John O'Doherty, and Raymond J. Dolan, "Automatic and Intentional Brain Responses During Evaluation of Trustworthiness of Faces," *Nature Neuroscience* 5 (2002): 277–83; Paul Ekman and Wallace V. Friesen, "Nonverbal Leakage and Clues to Deception," *Psychiatry* 32 (1969): 88–105.

105 **we notice these signals instinctively:** Miron Zuckerman, Robert Driver, and Richard Koestner, "Discrepancy as a Cue to Actual and Perceived Deception," *Journal of Nonverbal Behavior* 7 (1982): 95–100; Aldert Vrij, Katherine Edward, Kim P. Roberts, and Ray Bull, "Detecting Deceit via Analysis of Verbal and Nonverbal Behavior," *Journal of Nonverbal Behavior* 24 (2000): 239–63; Bella M. DePaulo, James J. Lindsay, Brian E. Malone, Laura Muhlenbruck, Kelly Charlton, and Harris Cooper, "Cues to Deception," *Psychological Bulletin* 129 (2003): 74–118.

106 **scientists have tracked his movements:** William A. Watkins, Joseph E. George, Mary Ann Daher, Kristina Mullin, Darel L. Martin, Scott H. Haga, and Nancy A. DiMarzio, *Whale Call Data for the North Pacific, November 1995 through July 1999: Occurrence of Calling Whales and Source Locations from SOSUS and Other Acoustic Systems* (Woods Hole, Mass.: Woods Hole Oceanographic Institution, 2000), 19; William A. Watkins, Mary Ann Daher, Joseph E. George, and David Rodriguez, "Twelve Years of Tracking 52-Hz Whale Calls from a Unique Source in the North Pacific," *Deep-Sea Research Part I: Oceanographic Research Papers* 51 (2004): 1889–1901.

106 **but also, perhaps, for navigation:** Allison K. Stimpert, David N. Wiley, Whitlow W. Au, Mark P. Johnson, and Roland

Arsenault, "'Megapclicks': Acoustic Click Trains and Buzzes Produced During Night-Time Foraging of Humpback Whales (*Megaptera novaeangliae*)," *Biology Letters* 3 (2007): 467–70.

107 **Andrew Revkin wrote about him:** Andrew Revkin, "Song of the Sea, a Capella and Unanswered," *New York Times*, December 21, 2004.

Chapter Six: Adaptability

110 **Everyone thinks of changing humanity:** Leo Tolstoy, "Three Methods of Reform," in *Pamphlets: Translated from the Russian*, trans. Aylmer Maude (Christchurch, N.Z.: Free Age Press, 1900), 29.

Chapter Seven: Integrity

132 **If you see a whole thing:** Ursula K. Le Guin, *The Dispossessed: An Ambiguous Utopia* (New York: Harper & Row, 1974), 190.

140 **take less than two hours:** Roger Panaman, "Behaviour and Ecology of Free-Ranging Female Farm Cats," *Zeitschrift für Tierpsychologie* 56 (1981): 59–73.

141 **symbols of their dominion and wealth:** Vernon N. Kisling, Jr., "Ancient Collections and Menageries," in *Zoo and Aquarium History: Ancient Animal Collections to Zoological Gardens*, ed. Vernon N. Kisling, Jr. (Boca Raton, Fla.: CRC Press, 2001), 1–47.

142 **to harbor their royal menageries:** Adolf Erman, *Life in Ancient Egypt*, trans. H. M. Tirard (1894; repr., New York: Dover Publications, 1971), 243.

156 **Integrity is never painless:** M. Scott Peck, *The Different Drum: Community Making and Peace* (New York: Simon & Schuster, 1987), 235.

Chapter Eight: Forgiveness

158 **Forgiveness is not an occasional act:** Martin Luther King, Jr., *Strength to Love* (New York: Harper & Row, 1963), 40.

168 **At its essence, forgiveness means:** Kris King, *My Heart Has Wings: 52 Empowering Reflections on Living, Learning, and Loving* (Austin: Bridgeway Books, 2009), 272.

170 **wreaks havoc in our bodies:** Jennifer P. Friedberg, Sonia Suchday, and Danielle V. Shelov, "The Impact of Forgiveness on Cardiovascular Reactivity and Recovery," *International Journal of Psychophysiology* 65 (2007): 87–94; Rebecca Stoia-Caraballo, Mark S. Rye, Keri J. Brown Kirschman, and Catherine Lutz-Zois, "Negative Affect and Anger Rumination as Mediators Between Forgiveness and Sleep Quality," *Journal of Behavioral Medicine* 31 (2008): 478–88; Everett L. Worthington, Jr., ed., *Handbook of Forgiveness* (New York: Routledge, 2005).

174 **Research proves that dogs' guilty looks:** Alexandra Horowitz, "Disambiguating the 'Guilty Look': Salient Prompts to a Familiar Dog Behaviour," *Behavioral Processes* 81 (2009): 447–52.

Chapter Nine: Presence

176 **There is one thing we can do:** Mark Van Doren, "On Being All There," *This Week Magazine*, December 7, 1952.

Chapter Ten: What Lies Beneath

202 **A human being is a part:** Albert Einstein, quoted in Rudolf v. B. Rucker, *Geometry, Relativity, and the Fourth Dimension* (New York: Dover Publications, 1977), 118.

211 **In the beginning of all things:** Letakots-Lesa (Eagle Chief), "Introduction to the Pawnee Songs," in *The Indians' Book: An Offering by the American Indians of Indian Lore, Musical and Narrative, to Form a Record of the Songs and Legends of their Race*, ed. Natalie Curtis Burlin (New York: Harper & Brothers, 1907), 96–98.

About the Author

For more that twenty-five years, Dr. Vint Virga has been a distinguished practitioner and leader in veterinary medicine, recognized for his insights into our relationships with animals. As a specialist in veterinary behavioral medicine and consultant to zoos and wildlife parks, his expertise spans the animal kingdom from dogs and cats to wild species such as leopards, gibbons, wolves, and giraffes. He has served as an advisor to leading U.S. corporations, professional associations, and animal welfare organizations, in addition to appearing as a featured guest on *ABC World News*, *National Geographic Explorer*, and PBS's *Nature*.

Dr. Virga writes a regular blog for *Psychology Today* and has contributed essays to *Conjunctions*, *Biographile*, *MindBodyGreen*, *Books for Better Living*, and *The Dodo*. In recognition of his writing, he's been awarded two MacDowell Fellowships and a Kate and George Kendall Fellowship. He lives in southern New England with his wife, daughter, and two Norwegian forest cats.

Printed in the United States
by Baker & Taylor Publisher Services